Jesus: Our City of Refuge

Dedication

To my sons Amir & Farid. May you always know and dwell in your one and true city of refuge: Jesus.

Special Thanks

My wife Nancy: for bearing with me while I was writing these past years, it is finally here.

Maged Zakher: for your great effort in editing this book, you are a true blessing. I am really so thankful and grateful.

Joe Fares & Sami Mufeed: for all the encouragement to pursue writing this book.

To all my friends who encouraged me along the way, appreciate and thankful for each one of you.

led away into a totally new land. They were literally stepping into the unknown.

Let me put it this way. I have been living all my life in Egypt. I got used to everything here, know all the rules even the unspoken ones between the people, all the shortcuts when traffic gets bad, the weather, the community, etc. Simply, I know my country. But what if I decided to immigrate to another country, Iceland for example?
I have no idea about anything there. Their laws, way of driving, culture, traditions, community….
I would be totally lost there so I need to know more about this new place where I am heading. It would be much better to read much about that country and understand its rules very well. An even better way is to sit with one of the citizens and listen to what he/she has to say describing their country. They would know better about all the details, big ones and small, spoken and implicit ones.

This is exactly what God was trying to teach the Israelites before they entered the promised land. He was trying to give them a blueprint of what kind of land they were heading to, so they would prepare themselves for the new rules there.

Even God was not that familiar to them. They had heard about Him and seen His mighty hands doing wonders in Egypt and delivering them out of the harsh bondage, setting them free for the first time in hundreds of years but they did not know Him.

Moses had this concern and when God commissioned him to go to Pharaoh, he asked Him this:
"Then Moses said to God, "If I come to the people of Israel and say to them, 'The God of your fathers has sent me to you,' and they ask me, 'What is his name?' what shall I say to them?" God said to Moses, "I AM WHO I AM." And he said, "Say this to the people of Israel, 'I AM has sent me to you.'" Ex. 3: 13,14

So Moses knew what to say to the people regarding God, and along the way, God gave him instructions and details regarding the new land He was leading them to. A new set of rules had to be in place for this new phase in their lives and God instructed Moses with every detail affecting their lives.

In our lives with God it is the same. When we surrender to Him and accept Him as our king, we are to enter a new kingdom with Him and we need to know more about it. The journey does not stop when I accept Jesus as my savior and embrace what He has done on the cross, becoming a living sacrifice for my sins.
The Bible does not preach about salvation only; it preaches about the kingdom. About how to live with God each day and not only the decision to follow Him.
Jesus often spoke about this kingdom so that we may be prepared to what is coming ahead.

The same applies to our daily lives with God. We were chained by our sins and destined for death, but Jesus came to deliver us and set us free through His death and resurrection. Anyone who accepted Jesus in their heart is starting a new phase in their life. A new land.
We are entering a new spiritual land, and we need to know more about its laws, rules and more importantly about the One who is leading us throughout this journey.
"Therefore, if anyone is in Christ, he is a new creation. The old has passed away; behold, the new has come." 2 Cor. 5:17

We need to know the laws of God's kingdom so that we may be able to live in it.

Every kingdom or nation has a set of rules to follow and all citizens of this nation should abide by and follow these laws.

Those citizens are also protected by such laws. God's laws of His kingdom were put to protect us and give us the best life ever.

The identity of any country is known by its flag / banner. If we have the banner of a certain country over us, then we abide by its laws.

When we see the banner we understand what set of laws by which this or that country is governed.

For example, when you see the flag of Britain, you will connect it with driving on the left side of the road. When you see the American flag, you will connect it with trading in US dollars.

The same applies with the kingdom of heaven. There are certain laws that govern this kingdom, but what is the banner of this kingdom to understand such laws?

The Governing Law

Let us examine what the Bible has to say about the banner over God's kingdom and from it we can conclude the governing law of this glorious kingdom.

It is written that "his banner over me was love." Song of Songs 2:4
The dominant law in effect here is the **Law of Love.** The banner is a symbol to the kingdom and God's kingdom is a kingdom where love rules, where God Himself is love and love never fails.

Love is the governing force in this kingdom. This is the true essence of this kingdom. God's love will always prevail and will always arise above any other force, spiritual or earthly.
"Mercy triumphs over judgment "James 2:13

So in order to better live in this kingdom and understand its dynamics, we need first to ask this question: What is this love like, then?

The Bible is full of passages speaking about this love but we must acknowledge that we will never grasp the whole dimensions of God's love for us.

We cannot contain or comprehend an infinite thing as God's love in finite vessels as our minds.

I believe that if we are eager and hungry enough, God will show us new depths of His love each day of our lives. Each day, we can witness a brand-new revelation and a deeper experience of His love towards us.

So let us examine a few traits of this love so as to have a glimpse of understanding of this governing force of our heavenly kingdom.

"love is strong as death....... Many waters cannot quench love, neither can the floods drown it" Song of Songs 8: 6,7

"I have loved you with an everlasting love; I have drawn you with unfailing kindness. "Jer. 31:3

This love is extremely strong and eternal. Nothing can stop God's love to us, even our own downfalls and sins, and this love does not change and is not affected by any circumstances.

This is simply God's nature. "God is love "
1 John 4:16

This strong love also offers us protection against any foe. He has this love as a high banner over our lives.

In wars, the banner signifies captured properties and lands from the enemy. You cannot raise your flag on another's property, only on property that you own or have reclaimed from your enemy.

Through His work on the cross, Jesus had reclaimed our lives from Satan. He paid the ultimate price, His blood, to buy us back form our enemy and then He raised His banner to proclaim this to everyone; to us, to the host of angels and to Satan and his evil spirits, that we are now God's own and no one can separate us from Him. His banner signifies that we are His. We belong to Him only.

"Who shall separate us from the love of Christ? Shall tribulation, or distress, or persecution, or famine, or nakedness, or danger, or sword? For I am sure that neither death nor life, nor angels nor rulers, nor things present nor things to come, nor powers, nor height nor depth, nor anything else in all creation, will be able to separate us from the love of God in Christ Jesus our Lord." Rom. 8:35, 38-39

This was the same case with the Israelites when they were delivered out of Egypt. They were once slaves and bound to the rules and laws of Egypt but they became free and had a new set of laws to govern their lives.

We are protected under His banner and no one can ever touch us while we are in that place.

And His banner is Love and under this glorious and powerful banner there is no fear, no condemnation, no shame, no hurts and no worries.
Only everlasting unchanged love from our heavenly Father.

Such love was the reason that God appointed such cities to be cities of refuge as we will discover later. But first let us marvel at the results of being under such a banner.

Chapter2

The Need of the Cities

Now we come to the question of Why? Why were these cities designed by God? Why were they important to the people of Israel?
These cities were appointed for anyone who by accident and unintentionally, caused another person to die. Such an accident was not a planned crime but still someone was killed and hence there must be a consequence.
The original meaning of unaware used to describe those who commit such crimes in Joshua 20:9 is: a mistake or inadvertent transgression, error, ignorance, unwittingly.

The killer in such case should flee to one of these cities right after that dreadful incident happened and stay there and never get out. There was no time to linger around, grab anything from his home or even bid farewell to family. Each minute he spent loose he was jeopardizing his own safety. These cities were meant as a safe place for anyone that killed another person accidentally so that any accuser cannot avenge from the killer.

In the Old Testament, relatives of the person killed had the right to avenge for his blood and kill the person who committed this crime even if it was by accident.

Blood must be shed in return. But as long as the murderer stayed in one of those cities, relatives of the deceased person cannot claim his blood or avenge from him. They cannot enter the city of refuge and kill him. This person was being protected by the city.

But if he gets out of that city and one of the dead man's relatives finds him, then this relative has the right to kill the murderer on the spot and avenge.

This is one of the earliest lessons that God wanted His people to learn; He is their true and only city of refuge.

We are all born under the sin and hence the devil has the right to come and demand our blood. It is in our human nature and we do not have any control over it. You see the Bible cannot contradict itself.

It is written "For the wages of sin is death" Rom. 6:23 and also "for all have sinned and fall short of the glory of God " Rom. 3:23

These verses make it very clear that all have sinned, including you and me. We were all born with this sinful nature within us.

These verses also show that that the wages of sin is death. It is a very clear statement and cannot be understood another way. It is straightforward. There is a price for such sin and the price is death. Blood must be shed and someone has to die.

Now it was God himself who set these rules in the first place but here comes a very hard dilemma; God is love and He loves all of us but at the same time, we have this nature of sin within us and hence, according to His law, we should die.
What shall a loving God do in order to prevent our death and in the same way keep His words upright?
We all need a way out so as not to pay the price for such sin which is death.

All our lives we seek redemption and safety form such destiny but we fail to find any. The price has to be paid and it is a very huge price. So, were these cities of refuge a temporary solution or a complete one?
We shall come to this point soon but first let us look more at the nature of these cities.

A city for anyone

"These six cities shall be for refuge for the people of Israel, and for the stranger and for the sojourner among them, that anyone who kills any person without intent may flee there. "
Num. 35:15

Moses was instructed by God to have these cities open to all people from all
nations. This was not something only for the Jews but for anyone who commits such an act and seeks protection.

Anyone could go to the cities of refuge and not only the Jews. This was a very early sign from God that the redemptive work of Jesus bound to come years later, will be for everyone who accepts Him and not only for the Jews.

"who desires all people to be saved and to come to the knowledge of the truth. " 1 Tim. 2:4

This is God's heart for everyone; that all should come to the knowledge of Him and accept the work of Jesus on the cross. Jesus would come for all mankind and not only a certain nation.

I am strong
In the strength of the Lord

"God is our refuge and strength, a very present help in trouble. " Ps. 46:1
More than 15 other times, the Psalms speak of God as our refuge. This is a truth that the Bible shouts very loudly so that we may hear and believe it and live accordingly.
Satan on the other hand is seeking our death, and that is why our only hope is to enter the city of refuge, the *true* and *everlasting* city; Jesus. If we go out of the City, then it is the accuser's right to claim our blood.

"That by two immutable things, in which *it was* impossible for God to lie, we might have a strong consolation, who have fled for refuge to lay hold upon the hope set before us."
Heb. 6:18
Allow me to quote what Adam Clarke said regarding this verse:

*"**We might have a strong consolation** - There appears to be an allusion here to the cities of refuge, and to the persons who fled to them for safety. As the person who killed his neighbor*

unaware was sure if he gained the city of refuge
he should be safe, and had strong consolation in
the hope that he should reach it, this hope
animated him in his race to the city; he ran, he
fled, knowing that, though in danger the most
imminent of losing his life, yet, as he was now
acting according to an ordinance of God, he was
certain of safety provided he got to the place.
It is easy to apply this to the case of a truly
penitent sinner. Thou hast sinned against God
and against thy own life! The avenger of blood is
at thy heels! Jesus hath shed his blood for thee,
he is thy intercessor before the throne; flee to
him! Lay hold on the hope of eternal life which
is offered unto thee in the Gospel!
Delay not one moment! Thou art never safe till
thou hast redemption in his blood! God invites
thee! Jesus spreads his hands to receive thee!
God hath sworn that he willeth not the death of a
sinner; then he cannot will thy death"
Adam Clarke

God is not a man to lie. When He says that the
true and only salvation is in Him then we will
never find any in other places.
"God is not man, that he should lie, or a son of
man, that he should change his mind. Has he
said, and will he not do it? Or has he spoken,

and will he not fulfill it? " Num. 23:19

We will never find salvation in power, money, relationships, sex, fame, material possessions, Salvation is to be found only in Jesus Christ.

"Take God's oath, take his promise; credit what he hath spoken and sworn! Take encouragement! Believe on the Son of God, and thou shalt not perish, but have everlasting life! "
Adam Clarke

Chapter 3

Final Words

We must always observe very well and take notice of one's final words before dying as these words usually summarize all the experiences and wisdom gained throughout years of living. With someone like Moses, with all that he had been through, experienced and got to know, we should really pay very close attention and take these words into consideration. It was as if he was putting the conclusion for the people of Israel and wanted them to remember these crucial facts.

These were Moses' final words.

"There is none like unto the God of Jeshurun, who rideth upon the heaven in thy help, and in his excellency on the sky. The *eternal God* is thy *refuge*, and underneath are the everlasting arms: and he shall thrust out the enemy from before thee; and shall say, Destroy them. Israel then shall *dwell* in safety alone: the fountain of Jacob shall be upon a land of corn and wine; also

his heavens shall drop down dew."
Deut. 33: 26-29

Now let us examine these verses.

Jeshurun means the Upright One. This name is a
symbolic name given for Israel
by God Himself describing an ideal character,
what it should be like.
When we follow God with all our hearts and
abide in Him, we are transformed into righteous
ones through His work in our lives.
God takes the old nature and transforms it into a
new one in the image of Jesus.

"He himself bore our sins in his body on the
tree, that we might die to sin and live to
righteousness. By his wounds you have been
healed." 1 Pet. 2:24

"For the kingdom of God is not a matter of
eating and drinking but of
righteousness and **peace** and *joy* in the Holy
Spirit. " Rom.14:17 (Emphasis added)

This verse will be referred to again later in this
book, but for this moment let us acknowledge
that God is the one who makes us righteous

through the sacrificial work done by Jesus on the cross.

We can also notice that these verses are like a summary to psalm 91 which we will be discussing later in this book.
But for a quick review, Moses acknowledges here that God is Israel's refuge, the one and only real city of refuge.

The eternal God, who will always be there for us whenever we need Him. This is our God whom we follow. He hurries for our rescue and there is no other god who can be like Him. He will deliver us from our enemies and protect us from any harm surrounding us.

After this, Moses states that there is a promise of blessings and abundant life that is awaiting those who dwell in this city of refuge, those who make the Almighty One their hiding place.
Jesus came to deliver us from sin and redeem us. He promised to be with us always, protecting us and blessing us in a bountiful way.

Please note these significant words in the above verses: Eternal God...refuge...dwell.
God is our true city of refuge and since God is

the only *Eternal God* thus we have this promise
of an *eternal* city of *refuge* as well. This city will
never change or cease being of this nature. It
will be always there for whoever runs towards it
and seeks its protection and *dwelling*.

This will lead us to the last of the words: dwell.
Dwell, as will be discussed later, is the key word
to unlock psalm 91 with all its richness and
blessings.
You see, when we dwell in the one and true city
of refuge, we will enjoy the company of the
Eternal God; the one who will hurry in our
defense, who will fulfill all our needs whether
physically or spiritually, the one who will
destroy all our enemies and make us trample
over them and crush their heads beneath our
feet. This is the life God promises us to live
when we choose to dwell in Him and not go
back to our old ways.

Chapter4

That Tribe

Now let us have a closer look at these cities. The first thing that catches our attention is the fact that all of these cities were Levite's cities.
So, what was special about this tribe that all six cities were cities belonging to it?
First thing to notice is that Levi did not inherit a certain piece of land. When the Israelites crossed the river Jordan into the promised land, each tribe had its share except the tribe of Levi.
This is what was written about Levi:

"Therefore Levi has no portion or inheritance with his brothers. The LORD is his inheritance, as the LORD your God said to him" Deut. 10:9

"And the LORD spoke to Moses, saying, Behold, I have taken the Levites from among the people of Israel instead of every firstborn who opens the womb among the people of Israel. The Levites shall be mine, for all the firstborn are mine. On the day that I struck down all the firstborn in the land of Egypt, I consecrated for my own all the firstborn in Israel, both of man and of beast. They shall be mine: I am the LORD." Num. 3: 11-13

"Take the Levites instead of all the firstborn among the people of Israel, and the cattle of the Levites instead of their cattle. The Levites shall be mine: I am the LORD." Num. 3: 45

God commanded Moses to separate that tribe and set it apart for God. They were to be the replacements of the firstborn who were to be given as a sacrifice for the people's sins.
Levi had only some cities designated and from these cities, the refuge cities were chosen,
We know that the priests were to be only from the tribe of Levi. The priest was the one who took the people's sin before God each year. In similar contest, the cities of refuge, being cities of the priests, bore the sin of the man slayer.

Those priests were to hold the nation's sins on them so that the people would live and not die. Once each year the high priest should enter into the Most Holy place in the tent and later the temple, and bearing the lamb's blood, they were to sanctify the people's sins so that no one should die in their sin.
But still someone had to die and blood had to be

shed for the forgiveness of these sins.
"Behind the second curtain was a second section called the Most Holy Place,…but into the second only the high priest goes, and he but once a year, and not without taking blood, which he offers for himself and for the unintentional sins of the people." Heb. 9: 3 & 7

"as the high priest enters the holy places every year with blood not his own" Heb. 9:25

"For the bodies of those animals whose blood is brought into the holy places by the high priest as a sacrifice for sin are burned outside the camp." Heb. 13:11

Now when the person who fled into such a city reaches it, he must eventually stand before the judge to determine if he is to be allowed to stay there or not.
"And he shall dwell in that city, until he stands before the congregation for judgment."
Josh. 20:6
Now the guilty person must stand before a judgment congregation to defend his case. If the judges believe that he committed that murder accidentally then he is free to stay in the city but never get out of it lest the avenger kill him.

In the same manner, we all must stand before The Judge someday, but the problem is this: there is a price that must be paid for sin and that price is Blood.

"For the wages of sin is death; but the gift of God is eternal life through Jesus Christ our Lord." Rom. 6:23

"and without the shedding of blood there is no forgiveness of sins." Heb. 9:22

So if the murderer stays in the city of refuge and is not killed by the avenger, whose blood is it going to be? Who will take this responsibility so that the sinner is truly free?

When Adam first sinned, sin entered the human race and as if it was in our genetic code, we inherited it from him.

"For if, because of one man's trespass, death reigned through that one man, much more will those who receive the abundance of grace and the free gift of righteousness reign in life through the one man Jesus Christ." Rom. 5:17

So, we all need a place where we can hide from the avenger and his blood-seeking right.

This means that this person cannot be free once

again unless he is dead. Was this the only way out?

Let us continue reading that same verse that we started this chapter with:

"And he shall dwell in that city, until he stands before the congregation for judgment, *and* until the death of the high priest that shall be in those days: then shall the slayer return, and come unto his own city, and unto his own house, unto the city from whence he fled."
Josh. 20:6

That person will be *Totally Free* only when the High Priest at that time *dies*. After that he can resume his normal life and return to his land, family and home.

But why? How come that someone's death sets another one free?

Most probably the high priest did not know this person and he even didn't volunteer to die instead of him.

But here is the beauty of the gospel revealed in such a way that knits together several parts in one striking and amusing passage. Let us explore it further:

"What the high priest was to the Levites, the Levites were to the nation.

On the Day of Atonement, therefore, all the sins of the nation came into his hand. On his death he was freed from the Law (Rom. 6:7; Rom. 7:1-4), and those whom he represented were freed also." (E. W. Bullinger)

"For he that is dead is freed from sin. " Rom. 6:7

So because the high priest was the one responsible to offer the sacrifice, he had to do this every year and yet neither him nor the people were completely free and he had to continue doing this. But when he is dead, that is when he is totally and finally free and hence those who were abiding in the city of refuge also would be. Someone actually died in their place and now they are free to resume their lives.

Jesus was the one who took our sins instead of us. He bore it on the cross.
So, by accepting this fact that Christ died instead of us and later resurrected from the dead, we would be truly freed from the blood punishment. This high priest was a symbol of Jesus and His work on the cross.

Hebrews chapter 9 beautifully describes this truth.

"But when Christ appeared as a high priest of the good things that have come, then through the greater and more perfect tent (not made with hands, that is, not of this creation) he entered once for all into the holy places, not by means of the blood of goats and calves but by means of his own blood, thus securing an eternal redemption. For if the blood of goats and bulls, and the sprinkling of defiled persons with the ashes of a heifer, sanctify for the purification of the flesh, how much more will the blood of Christ, who through the eternal Spirit offered himself without blemish to God, purify our conscience from dead works to serve the living God. Therefore he is the mediator of a new covenant, so that those who are called may receive the promised eternal inheritance, since a death has occurred that redeems them from the transgressions committed under the first covenant." Heb. 9: 11-15

Jesus went into the holiest place once and for all with His own blood, the only spotless lamb, so that we no longer would need another sacrifice. He was the final sacrifice and the ultimate one. Jesus is our high priest and because of His death, we are free at last just like the person who fled into the city of refuge was free upon the death of the high priest at that time.

Jesus' sacrifice was one that transcended all time barriers and included all humans who lived before Him and who will live until His second coming.
All we have to do is accept His work.

Chapter 5

The Cities

Now let us dig deeper into each city of the six cities of refuge and relate it to our day-to-day lives.

"And they appointed Kedesh in Galilee in mount Naphtali, and Shechem in mount Ephraim, and Kirjatharba, which *is* Hebron, in the mountain of Judah. And on the other side Jordan by Jericho eastward, they assigned Bezer in the wilderness upon the plain out of the tribe of Reuben, and Ramoth in Gilead out of the tribe of Gad, and Golan in Bashan out of the tribe of Manasseh. These were the cities appointed for all the children of Israel, and for the stranger that sojourneth among them, that whosoever killeth *any* person at unawares might flee thither, and not die by the hand of the avenger of blood, until he stood before the congregation." Josh. 20:7-9

First, we need to know that names in the Old Testament often have spiritual meanings therefore it is important to study each city's name as well as in which tribe it was located.

This will give us a new perspective to the meaning of these cities.

Now, there were three cities on mountains and three others were not but still all of them were built on high places so as to be seen from afar, but the first three were in mountainous areas and the last three were on plains. We will come back to this point after we have thoroughly studied each city, but allow me for now to just shed some light on the differences.

The first three represent the status where we are with God and He does inward work in us. He is cleansing us from within, freeing us and shaping our character after we first fled to Him. It is a very personal experience.

The next three are related to how we live in the world surrounding us and the things God is doing in our lives that are manifest to all around us.

So, let's start with the first city and at the end we will come back to this idea in more depth.

Kedesh: Holy Place. Holiness

"And they appointed Kedesh in Galilee in mount Naphtali "

The name Kedesh is derived from the Hebrew word "kaw-dash' " which means to be clean, purify, sanctify, consecrate.
Kedesh here in my opinion refers to holiness; being holy and consecrated, set apart to God alone.

Holiness simply means not tolerating sin. A holy heart is one that cannot live with sin. A heart that quickly repents and turns back to God. Holiness means the separation from sin and being consecrated to God alone.
Put it this way; imagine a bride on her wedding day wearing her white dress. This bride will easily notice any small stain and will not accept to continue with it. She cannot *tolerate* it. She will quickly try to find a solution to it.

Only God is capable of creating such a heart in us, a holy heart like His own. A heart that easily identifies sins and cannot tolerate or compromise with them.

"Follow peace with all men, and holiness, without which no man shall see the Lord" Heb. 12:14

Such a heart is also a consecrated heart. This means that I give God all rights in my life. I will not call the shots for my life but I give Him this right.

Samson was consecrated before his birth. "for behold, you shall conceive and bear a son. No razor shall come upon his head, for the child shall be a Nazirite to God from the womb, and he shall begin to save Israel from the hand of the Philistines." Judg. 13:5

Samuel too was consecrated as a child "But Hannah went not up; for she said unto her husband, I will not go up until the child be weaned, and then I will bring him, that he may appear before the LORD, and there abide for ever." 1 Sam. 1:22

It does not mean that you never sin, but it means that if you do fall in any type of sin, you will quickly feel it in your heart. You will feel that there is something wrong, something not functioning. Sometimes we are unaware of that sin, but you feel within you a sense of discomfort and a burden.

If you have been living with Jesus, you probably know that feeling.
It is a feeling from which you cannot run. It is simply the cry of the Holy Spirit against anything that may defile you or come in between you and God.

If you have never heard before of Jesus or even decided not to accept Him in your life, you still know what this means.
You are still struggling with this certain issue. You know it has control over your life though you try to show others and even yourself, that you have full control.
Perhaps, you have been unable to break through for years.
You have been wrestling with sin.

But the good news is there is hope. When you run into the city of refuge which is nowadays Jesus our real Savior, He will be able to free you from whatever is holding you captive. Be it lust, pride, envy, forgiveness or whatever bondage you were caught with.

Now let's take a look at the tribe in which Kadesh was located; Naphtali.

But before we proceed I would like to clarify a small point here.
We mentioned earlier that all the cities of refuge were Levites' cities. Cities dedicated for the priests and this is a symbol of Jesus' role as our true and living High Priest.
So how come is this city in Naphtali and all the other five cities are in different tribes?
This is simply because Levi didn't inherit land when they divided the promised land between the tribes. They had cities in different tribes and from those were the cities of refuge.
Levi's inheritance is God due to that tribe's specific and remarkable role.
Joseph also didn't inherit but his two sons did (Manasseh and Ephraim) thus making the calculation once back to twelve lands.

Naphtali means "wrestling"

God set Kedesh in Naphtalie as if He was trying to tell us that we do not need to struggle more or look away for someone to deliver us from our bondages. He is near and willing to cleanse us completely.

Now this is what I can call ABSOLUTE GRACE.
God is ALWAYS near. He is NEVER far from anyone who diligently seeks Him.

"You will seek me and find me, when you seek me with all your heart." Jer. 29:13

The same is with our spiritual lives. We need a solution for our sins so that we become holy like God and not accepting sins.
God said: "Come now, and let us reason together, saith the LORD: though your sins be as scarlet, they shall be as white as snow; though they be red like crimson, they shall be as wool." Isa. 1:18

You may feel like what you have done is really terrible and beyond repair or redemption.
You may say that you betrayed others, cheated on your spouse, got addicted, raped, lied, envied, killed, insulted, bribed.....and the list goes on.
You may have never heard of Jesus or know nothing about Him but you know down deep that you have been struggling with many habits that formed some sort of bondages throughout the years.
Maybe you have a drinking problem or have

been seduced in sexual relationships and cannot get out of them.

It could be that you always lie and manipulate to reach your goals or have been so deeply hurt by someone that you are trying to find satisfaction in other areas.

You end up blaming God for whatever happened in your life while trying to find a true meaning of your life.

But the common thing is whenever you try to break through by yourself you find yourself sinking more.

We are always wrestling and struggling to get rid of sin by ourselves but the true and only way is Jesus, the Only Holy One who in Him we can be holy and sanctified.

Before knowing God, we are all always struggling and wrestling to be free from all bondages that are hindering us from going forth with God.

We are like Naphtali, always wrestling but cannot get free.

This is like Quick Sand. If you enter into quick sand, you will find yourself sinking slowly. It even gets worse when you try to put some effort

to get out of it. Whenever you exert some effort, your best effort to get out of this slow and deadly trap, you will be sinking FASTER. It looks like a hopeless situation and some may feel like giving up and accepting their fate.
Do you know the only solution to get out of quick sand?
It is to lay still as if you are floating on water. All you need to do is Doing Nothing. Just surrendering and accept help from someone outside who can pull you out.

The same with the sins that we are wrestling against daily. When we try to fight them on our own, we get more trapped.

The problem is we are fighting against a spiritual power with our earthly power. We are trying to resist spiritual sins with our physical efforts and human will. We can never succeed.
We need to stop trying to free ourselves and surrender to the One who is able to do so. We need to sit still and surrender to Him.

"We have escaped like a bird from the snare of the fowlers; the snare is broken, and we have escaped!" Ps. 124:7
Only in Jesus, our true city of refuge, we can be

free, loose and able to be fruitful as well.

"and you will know the truth, and the truth will set you free." John 8:32

Now we come to another question; can a holy god accept sinful persons as we or should we try to cleanse ourselves first before opening our hearts to Him?
The truth that the Bible teaches us is that God accepts us as we are but He sanctifies us with His blood. He makes us holy as He is.
He is the one who can do such transformation. All we need to do is run to Him and abide in Him just as someone would run into the city of refuge.

God loves you today as He did before you were born.
He loves you so much that He sent Jesus His only Son to die on the cross so that you may have life, an abundant life.
You are a very special person in His sight; you are His son/daughter. Whether you believe this statement or not does not change this fact.

I may not believe in gravity but this does not change or cancel the fact that if I jump from the tenth floor I will drop down dead.

"For God so loved the world, that he gave his only Son, that whoever believes in him should not perish but have eternal life." John 3:16

Jesus is the only person that can help you to overcome any sin or bondage and become a holy person. Jesus walked the earth and faced every possible temptation we can face or think of so that He could help each and every one of us in whatever we are facing.

You may argue that things were different two thousand years ago and the surrounding temptations were not the same but I disagree.

"For because he himself has suffered when tempted, he is able to help those who are being tempted." Heb. 2:18

"For we do not have a high priest who is unable to sympathize with our weaknesses, but one who in every respect has been tempted as we are, yet without sin." Heb. 4:15

These two verses clearly state that Jesus was tempted in every aspect.

Sin is the same. Maybe the methods are different, but the temptation is the same.

Jesus is our High Priest who faced all possible sins and temptations and came out victorious. He even faced Satan face to face in the wilderness and overcame. He is the only person who ever lived or will ever live on this earth that has never sinned so He is the only person who can remedy us from our sinful nature.

Always beware of the reasons that are driving you into certain actions.
David's sin was not sleeping with Bathsheba and later killing her husband but lusting her in the first place.
Peter's sin was not complying with the Jews but it was fear of men.

The Promises to Naphtali:

There are two significant sets of promises to the tribes in the Old Testament;
One made by Jacob just before his death and the other by Moses, also before his death.
We will study both prophecies as the first was made in Egypt before getting out of it while the later was made just before entering the promised land.
These prophecies are not just some words of encouragement but those were
spoken with power and authority…they were divine words.

Now let's see what were the promises to Naphtali; a tired wrestler trying to get rid of the ropes holding him.

Jacob's Promise:

"Naphtali *is* a hind let loose: he giveth goodly words." Gen. 49:21

Naphtali is promised here to be like a deer, a female one. Don't you find it a bit strange for such a promise? Should Naphtali be happy when he hears it?

My perspective of deer mainly comes from National Geographic channel; they are predators' food. They are beautiful but too weak to win any fight and always end up being devoured by a lion or another predator. Moreover, Jacob is referring to a female deer. Most of us would tend to stereotype here and consider the females weaker than the males in general so this deer here is not a very good thing to promise someone who has been struggling for a long time that he will be like one. So why did Jacob use a hind here?

The hind loves freedom more than any other animal. The hind lives in the wild and loves to be free, to leap and run and enjoy being able to move in complete freedom.

Allow me to quote the following:

"The hind is a female red deer whose home is the mountains. The rear feet of the hind step in precisely the same spot where the front feet have just been. Every motion of the hind is followed through with single-focused consistency, making it the most sure-footed of all mountain animals. Now listen to how the Lord compares our

spiritual walk with the hind:
"He maketh my feet like hinds' feet, and setteth
me upon my high places." Ps. 18:33
"The LORD God is my strength, and he will
make my feet like hinds' feet, and he will make
me to walk upon mine high places." Hab. 3:19

Do you know that the Lord has some high places
for you? Places where the air is pure, the view
pristine, distractions are far below, and there
are paths just big enough for the two of you. It's
true that the climb up to the high places is a bit
more challenging than a level foot path in the
valley. But not if you've got those hinds' feet; the
hinds' feet equip you for the roughest terrain.
Can't you just smell that mountain air? What are
you waiting for?"
Hannah's Cupboard, a ministry of Barbra
Lardinais.

Can you see what God wants to offer you here?
He wants you to be free so that you go up in the
mountains and meet Him there.
This reminds me of the beautiful novel by
Hannah Hurnard "Hinds' feet on high places" I
really encourage you all to read it if you haven't.

Now on these high places this deer has very

special legs that are designed to be able to climb easily through these mountains. This gives the deer a huge advantage against all her enemies. This is a symbol of how we will be when we are set free from any bondages and be holy as God is. We will be like a deer set free from captivity to enjoy its freedom.

Don't try to break free yourself. All you need to do is trust in God and surrender to Him. He is the only one capable of breaking all the chains that were holding you all these years and set you free indeed.
We need to be in Him; our city of refuge.

Now we come to the second part of the promise: *giveth goodly words.*
I remember when I first met Jesus and decided to give Him my life and follow Him all my coming days. The feeling was that of real freedom and as if I was bound to something that kept me from moving freely but then I was set loose.

There was a burden on me that suddenly was lifted.
Moreover, I just felt I wanted to tell all my friends about what He has done to me, more

importantly about who He really was.
You see many of us grow up hearing about God
and learning about Him in church and school
and our homes, but it is quite different when we
have a real experience with Him.

You don't get to truly know someone by hearing
about them. You know a person by having a
relationship and living with them, and because
of this you will find yourself shouting the good
news to all those around you so that they would
know that person too. Just like the Samaritan
woman did at the well after her true and life-
changing encounter with Jesus.

"So the woman left her water jar and went away
into town and said to the people, "Come, see a
man who told me all that I ever did. Can this be
the Christ?"" John 4:28,29

Moses' Promise:

"And of Naphtali he said, O Naphtali, satisfied
with favor, And full with the
blessing of Jehovah, Possess thou the west and
the south." Deut. 33:23

Here Naphtali is accepted. He is sanctified so that he can stand before God. He is blessed from Jehovah directly.

God will pour over us his favor and blessings so that we may keep being holy before of Him.

We need to remain in our city of refuge and never depart so that we are always showered with this favor.

Because of the work of Jesus on the cross, we are now accepted before God and have favor in His eyes. Moreover, we are promised many blessings and abundance.

John Wesley said about this part:
"This is not to be understood of the place, that his lot should fall there, for he was rather in the east and north of the land; but of the pleasures and commodities of the west or of the sea, which were conveyed to him from his neighbor Zebulun; and of the south, that is, from the southern tribes and parts of Canaan, which were brought to him down the river Jordan, and both sorts of commodities were given him in exchange for the fruitful rich soil which he had in great abundance."

God is promising blessings and satisfaction of all your needs. He will use even other people to bless you and provide for you.

Shechem: Shoulder

"Come unto me, all ye that labour and are heavy laden, and I will give you rest." Matt. 11:28

"and Shechem in mount Ephraim. "

The word Shechem comes from shacham which means to be ready, forward, and diligent; hence Shechem resembles and symbolizes the shoulder, because of its readiness to bear burdens.

After submitting to God and trusting that He will sanctify us and make us holy as He is, He wants us to know that He will carry all our burdens. We often start our journey with God with zeal and joy but along the way we face many things that keep distracting us or hindering us from the path.
The devil sometimes allows us to keep going in the path but he throws such burdens on our shoulders so as to hinder us from the full potential that Christ wants us to be in.
Many times we continue following God while carrying some burdens. These burdens are usually heavy thus hindering us from two things:

1- Following God with the pace He wants us to keep.

Imagine entering a running race while carrying a heavy backpack on your shoulders; do you think you stand any chance of winning?
The same applies to our spiritual journey with God. We often go on this journey carrying many other stuff that we are not supposed to be carrying and thus hindering us from the full potential that God wants us to live in.

2- Carrying His fruits instead.

Now if we are busy carrying other burdens over our shoulders, we will not have the time, effort or ability to carry the fruits that our Master desires from us.
We are called to disciple nations and proclaim the good news, heal the sick and deliver the possessed. We are called to bear fruits and live His kingdom with its full authority and power.

"And other seeds fell into good soil and produced grain, growing up and increasing and yielding thirtyfold and sixtyfold and a hundredfold." Mark 4:8

So what are those burdens that we keep carrying around? Here are some:

- Guilt
  Unforgiving is a devastating force. It eats your inner soul like cancer if it is not dealt with promptly. One of its worst forms is unforgiving yourself.
  Many people have done such bad things in their lives or even caused harm to others that they cannot forgive themselves for what they have done.
  Even if their victims have shown them grace and forgiveness, they still have this guilt looming over their minds and crippling them from any true freedom.

  This can happen even to believers who have accepted Jesus as their savior but they still struggle with this heavy burden of guilt.

- False doctrines
  Many times we believe we need to do something to be qualified to receive God's grace. This is a bit ironic as grace is defined as receiving what we are not entitled to.
  Also there are some who, like the Pharisees in Jesus' time, love to put loads on people and thus

causing them to stumble and even turn away from such a life. We become burdened with many "must-do's" in order to obtain God's favor and grace or sometimes in order to be "accepted" in by churches. This is totally against what the Bible teaches us.

God's salvation is free for us. It is the costliest thing in the world but this price has been paid in full so we can simply receive such a gift.
No one could have ever paid such a price, to be the sanctifying lamb and carry all the sins of all humankind.

Do not carry any other burdens on your yoke except that of Jesus.

- Worries
  We live in a world that worries a lot about many things. We worry about our health, jobs, money, children, ministry and the list goes on.
  Most of the time, we have no control on what we worry about.

"And he said to his disciples, "Therefore I tell you, do not be anxious about your life, what you will eat, nor about your body, what you will put

on. For life is more than food, and the body more than clothing. Consider the ravens: they neither sow nor reap, they have neither storehouse nor barn, and yet God feeds them. Of how much more value are you than the birds! And which of you by being anxious can add a single hour to his span of life? If then you are not able to do as small a thing as that, why are you anxious about the rest?
Consider the lilies, how they grow: they neither toil nor spin, yet I tell you, even Solomon in all his glory was not arrayed like one of these.
But if God so clothes the grass, which is alive in the field today, and tomorrow is thrown into the oven, how much more will he clothe you, O you of little faith! And do not seek what you are to eat and what you are to drink, nor be worried. For all the nations of the world seek after these things, and your Father knows that you need them. Instead, seek his kingdom, and these things will be added to you." Luke 12: 22-31

Our Father promises to take care of EVERYTHING we need. We just need to focus on Him and His kingdom and He will satisfy all our needs according to His richness.

"And my God will supply every need of yours according to his riches in glory in Christ Jesus." Phil. 4:18

Jesus said: "Come unto me, all *ye* that labour and are heavy laden, and I will give you rest." Matt. 11:28
Jesus always meant what He said. He wants to carry all our worries and burdens;

All our financial worries, our anxiety over our kids, our worries regarding our future, work, relationships.
He wants us to have rest. Rest here in the original meaning means exempt.
As if God is saying that you will never carry this burden once more.
He wants us to be refreshed so as to be able to carry His fruits instead.

- Hurts & scars

Imagine an athlete preparing for a 100-meter race. He is fit and trained very well but has one problem, he has a wound in his leg, a deep wound that is still open and bleeding. Can such an athlete compete in this race, let alone have any chance of winning?

The same applies to our spiritual lives. Our hurts
and scars often hinder us from following God
where He leads us at the pace intended for us.
These will surely prevent us from bearing any
fruits as well.
I am not talking about physical hurts here but the
ones that are affecting our souls. Hurts from
being abused as a child, cheated upon from a
spouse, betrayed by friends and the list goes on.

Only Jesus can heal such deep scars and hurts as
He himself carried all such hurts on the cross.
He is the only person throughout history who
has experienced the pain that you are passing
through thus He is the only one who can help
you be free from it.

Jesus called us to carry only one thing over our
shoulders: "Come to me, all who labor and are
heavy laden, and I will give you rest. Take my
yoke upon you, and learn from me, for I am
gentle and lowly in heart, and you will find rest
for your souls. For my yoke is easy, and my
burden is light." Matt. 11: 28-30

Here Jesus is commanding us to carry only His

yoke and not any other thing.
So what is exactly is this yoke?

The word yoke that Jesus is speaking about
means in the original text to join or couple. Like
when you join two things in one task. It was
used to describe the yoke laid on two oxen so as
to carry out a certain work by the farmer.

Jesus simply wants to tell us to be with Him,
working with Him and carrying what's on his
heart to the world. This is the only yoke that we
should be carrying: Spreading the message of
salvation and living His kingdom on earth.

"who desires all people to be saved and to come
to the knowledge of the truth."
 1 Tim. 2:4

Pastor Bill Johnson mentioned in his book "God
is Good" that we often focus on the Gospel of
Salvation and neglect the Gospel of the
Kingdom.
You see, salvation is a major step in our lives
with God here on earth but it is never the end of
the journey.
The ongoing focus must be His Kingdom. We
are called to live God's Kingdom with all that's

in it here on earth with all what this Kingdom has to offer.

This is not a heavy yoke but at the same time very heavy from another perspective.
This yoke does not enslave us or pressure us in a way to crush us. It is not something that we carry against our will and are not free to break out of it.
It is on the other side a heavy one because we are being connected to the Father heart of God in His deep desire that all would be saved and live the kingdom life.
Such a yoke will make us humble before God and men.

We are not called to be heavy laden and bending underneath our heavy troubles and problems but we are called to stand strong and enjoy the feeling of the
removal of all the burdens from our shoulder. Jesus carries our burdens over His shoulders. He carries everything that troubles us, all our worries, fears and troubles. We can have our backs straightened at last and feel no pain, never look down again. He breaks every yoke from the devil that was put upon our shoulders, every bondage.

"You saw in the wilderness how the Lord your God carried you as a man carries his son all along the way you traveled until you reached this place." Deut. 1:31

On the cross He carried all of these so that we might be free in Him, and soar like eagles on high.

"I removed his shoulder from the burden: his hands were delivered from the pots." Ps. 81:6

Burden here means load. God does not want us to carry heavy loads over our shoulders. Loads that make us stumble and fall. Loads that hinder us from running with him.

In the famous book "The Pilgrim's progress", the Christian was carrying a heavy bag that made him weary and made his trip a very painful one until the day that his path led him to the cross. Gazing upon the cross, the heavy bag suddenly fell from his back and rolled down the hill and he never saw it again.

This is what God wants to do with us, He carried all our loads on the cross, on His shoulders, so that we may live freely.

"And it shall come to pass in that day, *that* his burden shall be taken away from off thy shoulder, and his yoke from off thy neck, and the yoke shall be destroyed because of the anointing." Isa. 10: 27

This is a work of the Holy Spirit. He alone can set us free from any yoke or bondage. It does not matter how big this yoke is or how many years you have been tied by it, the Holy Spirit is very powerful and He can and wants to break every yoke.

"For it shall come to pass in that day, saith the LORD of hosts, *that* I will break his yoke from off thy neck, and will burst thy bonds, and strangers shall no more serve themselves of him" Jer. 30: 8

"Stand fast therefore in the liberty wherewith Christ hath made us free, and be not entangled again with the yoke of bondage. " Gal. 5: 1

Remember that God promises that you will be exempted from any yoke but this does not mean that the devil will not try again to deceive you and lure you back under such burden or even new ones.

We must be on our guard and never leave our city of refuge; Jesus who carries our burdens on His shoulder and strengthen ours so as to carry His yoke with Him and bear fruits.

The Promises to Ephraim:

Shechem was from the tribe of Ephraim which means "double ash-heap: I shall be doubly fruitful"
Ephraim's name was a symbol of being abundantly fruitful. To be so, he should have nothing else on his shoulders, only the promised fruits.

Jacob's Promise:

Please be aware that Joseph did not inherit a piece of the promised land but his two sons, Ephraim and Manasseh did so the promises made to Joseph were also meant to his two sons.

"Joseph is a fruitful bough, a fruitful bough by a spring; his branches run over the wall. The archers bitterly attacked him, shot at him, and harassed him severely, yet his bow remained unmoved; *his arms were made agile by the hands of the Mighty One of Jacob,* from there is the Shepherd, the Stone of Israel, by the God of your father who will help you, by the Almighty who will bless you with blessings of heaven above, blessings of the deep that crouches beneath, blessings of the breasts and of the womb. The blessings of your father are mighty beyond the blessings of my parents, up to the bounties of the *everlasting hills*. May they be on the head of Joseph, and on the brow of him who was set apart from his brothers." Gen. 49: 22-26 The blessings here are described as limitless. The limits are the boundaries of the everlasting hills....there is no end to the blessings that Ephraim, who came from Joseph, would carry and no limit to the fruits he will bear.

Moses' Promise:

"And of Joseph he said, Blessed of Jehovah be his land, For the *precious things* of heaven, for the dew, And for the deep that coucheth beneath, And for the *precious things of the fruits* of the sun, And for the *precious things* of the growth of the moons, And for the chief things of the ancient mountains, And for the *precious things* of the *everlasting hills*, And for the *precious things* of the earth and the fulness thereof, And the good will of him that dwelt in the bush. Let the blessing come upon the head of Joseph, And upon the crown of the head of him that was separate from his brethren. The firstling of his herd, majesty is his; And his horns are the horns of the wild-ox: With them he shall push the peoples all of them, even the ends of the earth: And they are the ten thousands of Ephraim, And they are the thousands of Manasseh." Deut. 33: 13-17

Here Moses again repeats the phrase "everlasting hills". The promise here is that you will ALWAYS bear fruit to God.

This is part of His will for every child of His, that they bear fruit forever until the day that we meet Him in heaven.

And nothing will ever stop us from bearing these fruits as long as we are abiding in Jesus, our City of Refuge.

In this case, we will be **bearing fruits instead of burdens** because Jesus carried All our burdens on His shoulders on the cross.

And also note how many times the phrase "precious things" was repeated in these verses. The promise is that the fruits we will be bearing will be precious ones. As we stated earlier, Ephraim means Double Fruitfulness.

Instead of the slavery years, years that we were under heavy loads and bondages, God will transform our lives into fruitful ones.

And not only this but His promise is a Double blessing.

Hebron: Fellowship

"and Kirjatharba, which is Hebron, in the mountain of Judah. "

Hebron means association. Hebron is from the Hebrew word " חבר chabar" which means to associate, join, conjoin, unite as friends; and hence chebron, fellowship, friendly association. Hebron was also the place where Abraham for the first time had a home. The first place where he had a dwelling place.

"Then Abram removed *his* tent, and came and dwelt in the plain of Mamre, which *is* in Hebron, and built there an altar unto the LORD. "
Gen. 13:18
Dwell is a key word as we will discuss later, but for now let's just keep it in our minds, this is the place to dwell in and not just visit from time to time.

Hebron is also the most ancient of all the Cities of Canaan. After wandering about from place to place in the Land of Promise, pitching their tents and altars, it was here where the patriarchs had, for the first time, a settled home.

I believe this shows us that Jesus is our real Home where we can dwell and have true and deep fellowship together. Living with Him will make us praise Him more and more as we get to know Him better day by day and experience His everlasting love in a deeper level each day. David knew this divine secret, so he prayed this: "One thing have I asked of the LORD, that will I seek after: that I may dwell in the house of the LORD all the days of my life, to gaze upon the beauty of the LORD and to inquire in his temple. " Ps. 27:4

We are called to be Jesus' brothers/sisters and friends. We can always enjoy fellowship with Him while praising His highly exalted Name. We are called to be like Abraham; God's friends.

But being in friendship with someone means you need to spend time with this person and while you are spending that time, you will know how he feels, thinks, what makes him happy or angry. You get to know the slightest details of this person because you love him and care to be with him. Real friends share what's on their hearts to each other and don't keep secrets from one another.

My best friend always shares with me what is his next step in any of his aspects, work, relationships…. and he does this because he knows I care for him and would advise him honestly but more importantly because he wants to share.

Now look at what Jesus had to say about us: "No longer do I call you servants, for the servant does not know what his master is doing; but I have called you friends, for all that I have heard from my Father I have made known to you." John 15:15

Now here Jesus clearly states that He calls those who choose to follow Him and make Him Lord over their lives, friends. He shares everything with us, so this makes each one of us His best friend. Jesus wants to share what's on His heart with us. He loves to do so. He does not want to keep secrets from us.

Friend in this verse also has the same meaning as Associate.

Jesus puts us in the status and degree of a partner, friends working together and hence no secrets between them.

To prove this concept, Jesus takes the first step and declares to the disciples that He told them and made known all that He had heard from God the Father.

Also according to Thayer, the definition of friend in this verse is:
"one of the bridegroom's friends who on his behalf asked the hand of the bride and rendered him various services in closing the marriage and celebrating the nuptials"

Simply, Jesus is your BFF (Best Friend Forever)

But He wants you to know this and moreover, enjoy it. So what does it mean to be Best Friend Forever?

I guess we all had a best friend at some point in our lives. You had this very close friend with whom you spent more time than with other friends and sometimes more than your parents even. That friend with whom there were no boundaries in the relationship, no secrets, no jealousy but just pure friendship, devotion and love.

When I look at my relationship with my best friend over the years I can point out to some characteristics in that relationship so let's discuss these and examine how Jesus can be our best friend.

1- Availability

When we were young I used to spend almost each day with my best friend. We would go to the club or a movie together, spend time in each other's homes or just hang out doing anything. The days when we couldn't see each other, we would talk over the phone for at least an hour a day. It didn't actually matter what we said to each other but what mattered was just being there for each other.

As we grew up, busyness of life and responsibilities changed the way we live, and this available time got shorter and shorter. Sometimes you may even change your best friend according to the surrounding circumstances and due to the fact that this is a two-way relationship.

I still love and cherish my old friend but through the years I gained a new best friend. Though the new one is nowadays in a different country, we still have a very strong bond together.

But due to the fact that we are in the end humans, we cannot be there for each other all the time. Each has a family, work, ministry, hobbies and many things and even might be living in different countries with different time zones so things get a bit tough.

We have the will to be there but not always the time, physical power or merely the ability to do so.

Now Jesus wants to be your best friend and He promised this:
"And behold, I am with you always, to the end of the age." Matt. 28:20

This was His promise before he ascended to heaven. He will be with us ALWAYS. He is always available to us.
He is never occupied with other things. He promised to be there for us till the end of the age and then in heaven with Him as well.

I remember several years ago I woke up to a phone call from my sister in the middle of the night. She just heard that our second cousin who lived in Canada just suffered a severe concussion while playing soccer and there was something serious with his memory.

She had just heard the news and wanted to share this with me. After she hung up, I just sat in my bed not knowing what to do. I wanted to tell my mom but thought it was a really bad idea to wake her up just to tell her this and let her worry all night as I did.

Then while I sat alone in the darkness of my room I felt God whispering in my heart that He is there with me in that room and I can cast that burden on Him.

As soon as I prayed about it and laid it all to Him, I just felt ease and rest. The kind of rest when you are holding a secret or burden and you just spill it out to the one you trust the most.

I learned that night that Jesus is always there for me whenever and wherever I want to talk to Him. In fact, He is the ONLY one who will always be there for me.

2- Honesty

Honesty is not an easy trait. Not all can welcome honest advice or opinion but a true friend will always tell you the honest answer.

Sometimes you ask your friend for advice in a certain situation and you want him or her to agree with your opinion so that you would feel more confident and comfortable in the decision you are about to take, but a real friend will say the truth and give their honest advice even if they know it will upset you.

I would rather let my best friend be upset with me for a while than deceive him with false advice or opinion just to make him happy for a short period.

Other times you find yourself, out of your deep love and care towards your friend, obliged to confront him with any wrong he has done, even rebuking him.
This is done in a loving and humble way and for his sake in the first place.
It is because I deeply care for him that I cannot tolerate the harm he is inflicting on himself and others.

"Better is open rebuke than hidden love."
Prov. 27:5

God does the same with us. He is always there as we discussed earlier and He will always give us the most true and sound advice when we seek it.

But be careful. There is a small difference if you are just seeking a blessing to your already-made decision or you are really open to whatever He will guide you to.

Sometimes we are desperate to do or have something and we just need to hear God say OK. Maybe it is a relationship, a choice at work, an open door for ministry.
Please remember that Jesus is your best friend, so He will never cheat you but will tell you the truth always. It is up to you to take His advice or not.

Be sure that when He speaks to you about certain things in your life that need to be changed, He is doing this out of His love for you. He never condemns you but is always there as your best friend.

3- Fun being with

Now who would want to be with someone who won't enjoy their company or can't have fun together?

This is a huge part of having a best friend, that you can have a pleasant time together and enjoy it. You look forward to being with your best friend because you do have a good time together. You laugh together, talk together, have many common things, share secrets and can easily spend hours or days without any sense of feeling bored. It is fun being with this person.

The same applies to our relationship with Jesus. I believe the disciples had a really good time with Jesus alone. It was not only a mentor-disciple relationship, but I believe it was a friend-friend relationship.
Yes, the disciples were with Jesus in His sermons, while He was performing marvelous miracles but I also believe they had the best times of their lives with Him.

4- Understands me very well

Have you ever been in this situation that by looking into someone's eyes you knew instantly what precisely he was thinking about?
Well, true friends build such a trait and practice it.

My best friend knows what I like and dislike, which food I love, my hobbies and interests and even what I think about or plan to do.

This comes about by being close to each other for a long time and caring for and loving each other. You can find this in many married couples who due to their love and closeness to each other, develop such a capability to understand the eyes language.

You see, just being close to someone does not make you best friends. You must be caring and loving to be with this person.

As I just mentioned, one of the best examples can be found in marriage. You and your spouse should be best friends. You spend a great deal of time together, do things together, love and care for each other. This will result in being friends in a deeper and intimate level each day.

Now Jesus knows everything about you simply because He is the one who created you in the first place. He is the one who loves you most in the whole world and wants to spend ALL of the time with you. And it does not stop here as Jesus wants you to know His heart very well and know

His will and thoughts just like He knows what is on the Father's heart.

5- Being myself with

When you are with your best friend, you can be completely open with him.
There is no need to wear any masks or pretend to be someone else. No need to try to hide any feelings or make things look better.
It is OK to be vulnerable with your best friend.

Actually, it is a good thing. We all need someone who ACCEPTS us as we are and we can be ourselves with them. We don't need to make all things better. We can just come as we are knowing that this person loves and accepts us the way we are.
We know that our friend will not condemn us for any wrong we have done but rather show love and support. So just imagine if this friend is Jesus Himself. Accepting you as you are and welcoming you always to come to Him.

Jesus is the only person whom we can be completely vulnerable and open with.

He never condemns us but rather takes us in His embrace so that we feel loved and secure.

"There is therefore now no condemnation for those who are in Christ Jesus. " Rom. 8:1

This does not mean that He accepts our sins but it means He does not condemn or accuse us, that is the work of the devil, but He longs to have us in his embrace and rid us of all our sins once we repent just like the father did to his prodigal son.

"But while he was still a long way off, his father saw him and felt compassion, and ran and embraced him and kissed him" Luke 15: 20

6- Defend each other

True friends always stick together. You have probably heard the saying "A friend in need is a friend indeed"

When your best friend is in a tough situation or someone is attacking him, you find yourself there to defend and stand by him. If he is passing through a difficult time in work, relationships, sickness or any other situation, you are there for him.

You have his back as he would have yours if needed.

The thought itself that there is someone standing by you always, backing you and just being there for you is very encouraging and relieving.

Jesus does the same for us. He is ALWAYS there to protect us and have our backs. Many times we cannot see this protection or feel it but trust me He is there for you always.

He sends His angels for our protection and He always keeps His eyes on us, day and night.

"For thus said the LORD of hosts, after his glory sent me to the nations who plundered you, for he who touches you touches the apple of his eye:" Zech. 2:8

What a privilege and honor to be called Jesus' best friend. If we think for a while we would soon realize that this is all by God's grace. We have nothing at all in ourselves, but it is all God's love and grace that make us His friends.

Promises to Judah:

Judah means "praised" so let's examine the promises made to him.

Jacob's Promise:

"Judah, your brothers shall praise you; your **hand** shall be on the neck of your enemies; your father's sons shall bow down before you.
Judah is a lion's cub; from the prey, my son, you have gone up. He stooped down; he crouched as a lion and as a lioness; who dares rouse him?
The scepter shall not depart from Judah, nor the ruler's staff from between his feet, until tribute comes to him; and to him shall be the obedience of the peoples. Binding his foal to the vine and his donkey's colt to the choice vine, he has washed his garments in wine and his vesture in the blood of grapes.
His eyes are darker than wine, and his teeth whiter than milk. " Gen. 49: 8-12

Moses' Promise:

"And this is the blessing of Judah: and he said, Hear, LORD, the voice of Judah, and bring him unto his people: let his **hands** be sufficient for him; and be thou an help to him from his enemies." Deut. 33:7

Now Jesus came from the tribe of Judah and we have here the promise of Jesus Himself. These promises are a prophecy about Jesus Himself. Judah was promised that our true friend would come from him. There will always be praises due to the fact that Jesus is with us always, close like a best friend.

When we are associates with God, we have all His power and authority and He will make our hands strong in battle. Remember that Jesus is calling you to be His Best Friend.

Bezer: Strong Hold

"And on the other side Jordan by Jericho eastward, they assigned Bezer in the wilderness upon the plain out of the tribe of Reuben."

Bezer comes from the word "batsar" which means to restrain, enclose, shut up, or encompass with a wall, a fortified place, a fortress and hence the goods or treasure thus secured.

It also means an inaccessible spot. There is no way ever an enemy can penetrate its walls or go inside.

The person who fled to the city of refuge was in complete safety. These cities were strongholds to ensure the protection of those inside. They were fortified cities that none can penetrate. Stronghold always signifies a very difficult place to conquer and because of this trait, treasures and precious things were often hidden in such cities.

So, what happens when we flee to Jesus and remain in Him?

We have the ultimate protection against all our enemies. We are in the most secure place in the whole universe: in Jesus. No enemy can penetrate His divine protection around us. David knew this truth very well:

"The LORD is my rock and my fortress and my deliverer, my God, my rock, in whom I take refuge, my shield, and the horn of my salvation, my stronghold."
Ps. 18:2
We are only safe when we abide in Jesus.

Now this city, Bezer, was "in the wilderness" The wilderness always speaks about a difficult time or trials. The wilderness is often a desolate place, lonely and fearful one. Please be aware that all of us at some point will pass through a dessert in our lives. Jesus was in the wilderness when Satan came to tempt Him.
It will be a tough time where you may feel that you are all alone, hopeless and ready to give up, but please remember that as long as you abide in Jesus, your city of refuge and your stronghold, you will eventually come out of that dessert.
And not only will you survive but you will come out stronger than you started, with increased faith and complete trust in Jesus.

This is what indeed happened to me. I tested positive for COVID-19 and after a time of self-isolation in my house, things began to take a downward curve and my health began to deteriorate. Eventually I had to go to a hospital where I spent 24 days. Those days were the toughest and many times I felt I could not take it anymore and was about to just give up everything but God was very faithful to me. Not only was I miraculously healed but God sustained me at this tough time. He was like the city of refuge surrounding me.

So, the next time you find all your surroundings are not going well and as if everything is falling down on you, just trust in God and His everlasting love and protection. You have this city of refuge in the middle of each wilderness you will pass through. You will never be alone. No fear when we are with Jesus for He protects us. He is the Son of God in whom is our safety.

Also, please note that in these cities of refuge, no weapons of any kind were allowed to be made or carried inside. Those who possessed any had to surrender them. They had to rely on the nature of the cities as strongholds and a place of protection for them rather than on carnal weapons.

Jesus is our only defender. We must surrender anything that we depend upon.

We may be depending upon our money, wisdom, relationships, authority, family, etc., but all of these will never give us the real safety; only Jesus can.

Moreover, inside these cities the treasures were secured. This made sense as according to the nature of such cities, they were the safest place to keep any treasures knowing they were in the most secure place.

And guess what; YOU are this treasure. Each one of us who decided to follow Jesus and make Him our city of refuge are His most precious treasure.

Jesus paid the highest price ever for YOU. He paid His blood and His life so that we might live.

We have been BOUGHT from sin to have everlasting life.

We are priceless.

If you combine all the money, gold, silver, diamonds, precious stones and anything that has value on earth, it will never rise to a fraction of your price and value.

"You were bought with a price." 1 Cor. 7:23

We are God's treasure and He will take good care of us and will make sure that all measures are taken so that none might steal us from Him or harm us in any way as long as we remain in Him.
But it is OUR choice. If we decide to walk out of the city of refuge, then we are exposed to all weapons and assaults of the enemy and we lose our protection.

Promises to Reuben:

Reuben means "behold a son". He was the firstborn son of Jacob.

Jacob Promise:

"Reuben, you are my firstborn, my might, and the first fruits of my strength, preeminent in dignity and preeminent in power. Unstable as water, you shall not have preeminence, because

you went up to your father's bed; then you
defiled it—he went up to my couch!"
Gen. 49: 3,4

Moses Promise:

"Let Reuben live, and not die; and let not his
men be few." Deut. 33:6

Reuben here is blessed first with might and
strength hence Bezer is from his tribe to
symbolize this strength and power.
Also preeminence means excellency. Reuben
was blessed with excess and abundant power. It
also means a superior power.
This is the character of our city of refuge, it is
superior in power and even has abundance of it.

But then Jacob wasn't pleased with Reuben as
he defiled his father's bed.
This sin had to linger with Reuben making him
unstable until Moses gave him a new blessing.

Moses' blessing here is a bit strange. A blessing
to "live and not die"
How is this possible?
Well, let's take these blessings unto our lives:
we are promised security and might but we may

have some lingering sin, sin that leads eventually to our death.

But when we enter into covenant with God and hide in our city of refuge, we will truly live and not die. We have the everlasting life.

"And this is eternal life, that they know you the only true God, and Jesus Christ whom you have sent." John 17:3

Also remember this; Reuben means behold a Son and Jesus is the Son of God.

"And we know that the Son of God has come and has given us understanding, so that we may know him who is true; and we are in him who is true, in his Son Jesus Christ. He is the true God and eternal life." 1 John 5:20

"Since then we have a great high priest who has passed through the heavens, Jesus, the Son of God, let us hold fast our confession" Heb. 4:14

Like Reuben, Jesus is also the firstborn.

"who is the image of the invisible God, the firstborn of all creation" Col. 1:15

"For those whom he foreknew he also predestined to be conformed to the image of his Son, in order that he might be the firstborn among many brothers." Rom. 8:29

Jesus is our strength and might and in Him we will live forever.

"I am the resurrection and the life. Whoever believes in me, though he die, yet shall he live, and everyone who lives and believes in me shall never die. Do you believe this?" John 11: 25,26

Ramoth: Exaltation

"and Ramoth in Gilead out of the tribe of Gad "

Ramoth comes from the Hebrew word " ראם
raam "which means to be raised, made high or
exalted, and hence Ramoth, high places,
eminences.

Who could have believed that a fugitive running
from punishment would so far be blessed with
all these blessings? How come that we as sinners
are treated in this way by a loving God? He
offers abundant blessings to anyone who will
flee from sin and run into the one and eternal
city of refuge: Jesus.

Not only are we cleansed from our sins and
sanctified and made holy.
Not only are we free from all bondages and set
loose to be fruitful.
Not only are we showered with such grace to
have the right and privilege to enter into a
relationship and fellowship with our God.
Not only are we promised complete protection
and safety.
We are also promised here victory and an
exalted place to reign with our loving Father.

"Therefore God has highly exalted him and bestowed on him the name that is above every name " Phil. 2:9
"And Jesus came and said to them, "All authority in heaven and on earth has been given to me " Matt. 28:18

God has exalted Jesus on high and set Him above all rulers and authorities and by surrendering our lives to Him, we are to rule with Him and abide in that high place. God wants to raise us up to His own place of authority so that we may utilize this power that He gave us to bring heaven on earth.
Jesus is THE KING and we are to rule with Him as kings. We should never accept or be satisfied with anything smaller than this role and place.

We need to perceive this new nature that God bestowed on us. We are more than conquerors and we rule with Him from the heavens.
"Truly, I say to you, whatever you bind on earth shall be bound in heaven, and whatever you loose on earth shall be loosed in heaven "
Matt. 18:18
This is a huge thing to believe, and very challenging to practice. We are transformed

from fugitives and outcasts to rulers with power. We are to change the reality around us and never accept it as it is.

We are commissioned to bring the kingdom of heaven on earth with all that this kingdom has to offer:
Healing for the sick.
Freedom for the prisoners.
Joy for the sad.
Rest for the weary.
Hope for the hopeless and the list goes on.

Remember it is never we who do such things. This is all done by the Holy Spirit living within us when we give Him all control over our lives and obey His gentle voice and direction. The disciples did not have power of their own but when they were filled with the Holy Spirit and surrendered their will to His, they went around and changed the whole world preaching the good news and doing wonders and miracles. They were bold in front of their adversaries as they stood and practiced their exalted position in Jesus.

Kings do not sit and worry and succumb to the surroundings. Kings rise up and act from their place of authority and power to change the reality surrounding them.

When Jesus ascended into heaven after the resurrection, He gave us His power and placed us with Him in the most high and exalted place to exercise our authority here on earth as He did while He was on earth.

So it is our duty to go out and heal the sick in His name, set free the demon-possessed ones, preach the gospel of the kingdom and do even more than Jesus did on earth.

"Truly, truly, I say to you, whoever believes in me will also do the works that I do; and greater works than these will he do, because I am going to the Father." John 14:12

Paul and Peter did miracles that Jesus had not done before and we also are called to do so. This is simply His promise to us so we need to act upon this knowing that whatever He promised, He is capable to make come true.

These are all some nice encouraging words but the main challenge is that we are called to live this life and not just read about it and be encouraged and hope that someday we will see many get healed and set free.

Well, the sick will not get healed by themselves nor the prisoners will be set free from their sins by their strength. It is up to us to practice our rights and authority given to us by Jesus as long as we abide in Him, to make these things a reality and not just wishful thinking.

I once was in an orphanage for kids with special needs and found myself saying to God "Why don't you do anything to help these kids and cure them? "
I immediately heard God saying "What did YOU do about them? "
I suddenly realized that we are to do what Jesus used to do when He was on earth. This is now our responsibility and role.
It is not an Option but a Responsibility.

Moreover, God has equipped us to do these things so we actually have no excuse. When we abide in Jesus and are filled with the Holy Spirit, He will guide us and help us accomplish all these things.
Remember that these were Jesus' last words before ascending to heaven:
"And Jesus came and said to them, "All authority in heaven and on earth has been given to me. Go therefore and make disciples of all nations, baptizing them in the name of the Father and of the Son and of the Holy Spirit, teaching

them to observe all that I have commanded you. And behold, I am with you always, to the end of the age." Matt. 28: 18-20

"And he said to them, "Go into all the world and proclaim the gospel to the whole creation. Whoever believes and is baptized will be saved, but whoever does not believe will be condemned. And these signs will accompany those who believe: in my name they will cast out demons; they will speak in new tongues; they will pick up serpents with their hands; and if they drink any deadly poison, it will not hurt them; they will lay their hands on the sick, and they will recover." Mark 16: 15-18

We all get encouraged by these words, but the problem is we seldom act upon them. We do not practice these rights of ours mainly because of two things:
- We are afraid to fail and get embarrassed.
- We do not know our authority and responsibility.

- Fear of failing:

One of the main reasons we are not living to the standard that God wants us to be in is our fear. We have many questions; what if the person I pray for does not get healed? What if what I said to another person during prayer did not happen? What if I heard God wrong in the first place? Do you notice a common thing in these questions? It is the word "I "

You see, most of the time we are focused on ourselves and care only about our appearances. We are afraid that WE might fail or WE get embarrassed.
WE want everything to be perfect and do not want to be looked at in a lesser way. It is all about OURSELVES and not God anymore.
It is at this point that we fail. We are controlled by fear and the care for our own image more than what God commissioned us to do.
Please remember that "There is no fear in love, but perfect love casts out fear. For fear has to do with punishment, and whoever fears has not been perfected in love." 1 John 4:18

But what if we failed once? What if my faith has been shattered and I cannot stand again once more?

I once read a quote saying "Mistakes are good. They are proof of learning "

So do not be afraid to make mistakes. God never condemns us. He loves us and will train us as Jesus did with his disciples.

The only way to be free from the spotlight on the self is the cross. Paul said it in the simplest and deepest way:

"I have been crucified with Christ. It is no longer I who live, but Christ who lives in me. And the life I now live in the flesh I live by faith in the Son of God, who loved me and gave himself for me." Gal. 2:20

We need to die to our selves and human nature so that Jesus may live in us the victorious life in us. I once heard this quote that summarizes this idea: "When your soul is on the throne of your heart, Jesus is on the cross. When your soul is on the cross, Jesus is on the throne of your heart. " When we choose to die to our selves on the cross with Jesus and make Him lord, the focus will no longer be on us. The spotlight will be shifted from us to HIM.

- Lack of knowledge

The other main reason is we simply do not know
that we have the authority, power, capability and
responsibility to do such things.
"My people are destroyed for lack of
knowledge" Hos. 4:6
Remember that ignorance would result in
robbing you of very precious things God has for
you. When we receive Jesus as king in our hearts
and abide in Him as our city of refuge, we are in
the SAME place where He is now, the exalted
place in heaven. So I want to encourage each
one of you and myself as well to trust God and
accept our role as kings and priests seated with
Jesus.

Imagine a soldier in the battlefield who does not
know that he has a powerful weapon with him or
does not know how to use it. He will be really
missing big chances. We need to spend time
with God and His word, understand our rights in
Jesus and our roles assigned from God and learn
how to practice them in His divine power.

Promises to Gad

Gad means "troop" a group of soldiers or a cavalry commanded by a captain.

Jacob's Promise:

"Raiders shall raid Gad, but he shall raid at their heels. " Gen. 49:19
In this verse Gad is promised that he will FINALLY conquer his enemies.
Though his enemies will raid him first, the final victory will be his.
The same is with us. Though we are all born in sin and already beaten by Satan yet we have the promise of the ultimate victory in Jesus Christ and through His blood and His work on the cross.

"O Death, where are your plagues? O Sheol, where is your sting?" Hos. 13:14
This is the Exalted place that God promises us to be with Him in. If we keep our faith in the midst of the wilderness and abide in Jesus, our reward shall be to sit with Him and rule from the high places, to raid our spiritual enemies and conquer them.

This is a repayment for every time the devil robbed us from something.
Robbed our health, possessions, relationships...everything. God will set us up in this exalted place to rule as kings.

Moses' Promise:

"And of Gad he said, Blessed *be* he that enlargeth Gad: he dwelleth as a lion, and teareth the arm with the crown of the head. And he provided the first part for himself, because there, *in* a portion of the lawgiver, *was he* seated; and he came with the heads of the people, he executed the justice of the LORD, and his judgments with Israel. " Deut. 33:20,21
In the Mosaic blessing, not only are we victorious but we are seated in the place of those who set the laws. We are to be with the heads of the people hence nowadays we are to be with Jesus Christ around His throne.
We have the privilege to be in this high and exalted place of power and authority as Jesus is right now.

All authority has been given to Jesus after His resurrection and to us as well after we have fled into Him and dwelt in our true city of refuge.

Again let us consider this verse: "Truly, I say to you, whatever you bind on earth shall be bound in heaven, and whatever you loose on earth shall be loosed in heaven. " Matt. 18:18

We have the right and authority to bind and loose things here on earth.

To bind Satan's power over people. To set loose healing and blessings.

To bind evil schemes over individuals and nations. To set loose those who are captives. To bind evil spirits.

To act just like Jesus when He was on earth, to go around healing the sick, setting prisoners free and proclaiming the good news of the kingdom's gospel.

"The Spirit of the Lord GOD is upon me, because the LORD has anointed me to bring good news to the poor; he has sent me to bind up the brokenhearted, to proclaim liberty to the captives, and the opening of the prison to those who are bound; to proclaim the year of the LORD's favor, and the day of vengeance of our God; to comfort all who mourn; to grant to those who mourn in Zion— to give them a beautiful headdress instead of ashes, the oil of gladness instead of mourning, the garment of praise instead of a faint spirit " Isa. 61: 1-3

This was a prophesy regarding Jesus but this is actually what we should be busy doing right now. We are God's ambassadors and we should carry on His work.

I had the privilege of meeting some ambassadors in my life and chatting with some even in private meetings. I remember it was quite an experience that will be in my memory for a long time. My wife also worked in an embassy for some time so we got accustomed to many protocols and actions that are related to the work of an ambassador.

Any ambassador is a representative of his/her country. The ambassador speaks in the name of that country and all his views and decisions are the country's as well. He doesn't speak of himself. He doesn't speak his own opinion but as he receives from the high authorities back in his home country so he does.

One of the privileges in my opinion of being an ambassador is that he does not have to worry about where he should live and how to provide his daily needs and family requirements, his country is RESPONSIBLE for all of these in the most satisfying way.

His only job is to receive instructions and execute them and be a REPRESENTATIVE of his country's king or president.

The same in my opinion applies to our lives here on earth. It is written:
"Therefore, we are ambassadors for Christ, God making his appeal through us. We implore you on behalf of Christ, be reconciled to God. "
2 Cor. 5:20
Alfred Barnes explains this verse as follows:
"An ambassador is a minister of the highest rank, employed by one state at the court of another, to manage the concerns of his own state, and representing the dignity and power of his sovereign. He is sent to do what the sovereign would himself do if he was present. They are sent to make known the will of the sovereign. At all times, and in all countries, an ambassador is a sacred character, and his person is regarded as inviolable. He is bound implicitly to obey the instructions of his sovereign, and as far as possible to do only what the sovereign would do were he himself present. "
God has appointed us as ambassadors for His kingdom to go out and declare His appeal and

will to everyone and to reconcile people back to Him.

Remember that if there is a strong country in the world then its ambassador is considered and dealt with in the same manner of strength and respect. Same applies to us. We represent the most powerful kingdom in all of the universe so we should act from the highest and most exalted position.

God is calling and summoning all people to get back to Him and have eternal life and it is our duty and privilege to share this message. We are also to proclaim His kingdom's gospel.

Again I quote Alfred Barnes:
"We are ambassadors for Christ, as we are sent to do what he would do if he personally was present. We are simply to urge, explain, state, and enforce the terms on which God is willing to be reconciled. We should not go to promote our own welfare; not to seek honor, dignity; but to transact the business which the Son of God would engage in if He personally is on the earth. "

We are to act in a way similar to Jesus if He was living right now with us.

Hence we are not to worry about where we will live, what to eat, which schools shall our children go to, how to handle all responsibilities as all of these are taken care of by our Kingdom. "No soldier gets entangled in civilian pursuits, since his aim is to please the one who enlisted him. " 2 Tim. 2:4

Moreover, we are to imitate Christ and allow God to speak through us as Jesus did.
"Do you not believe that I am in the Father and the Father is in me? The words that I say to you I do not speak on my own authority, but the Father who dwells in me does his works."
John 14:10
We are to receive what's on God's heart and share it. We are to focus on our mission only and allow God to shine through us to whoever we are living with.

Let us live as we are called to, Ambassadors to God and citizens of the heavenly kingdom.

Golan: Joy

"and Golan in Bashan out of the tribe of Manasseh. "

Golan comes from the Hebrew word " גלה galah "which means to remove, transmigrate, or pass away; hence Golan, a transmigration or passage. Some derive it from " גל gal " which means to rejoice, hence Golan, rejoicing or exultation. It also means "their captivity: their rejoicing" while Bashan means "fruitful" and it was a very fertile land.

As the saying goes, the best is reserved to the last. After all of these blessings and transformations now we have the final cherry on top of the cake.
We are promised Joy. After years of captivity and pain we are to rejoice and find the real and everlasting joy that comes only from our Lord.
In this world we are all seeking true happiness and joy but we seek these in ways other than the only true way.
It is written: "for my people have committed two evils: they have forsaken me, the fountain of living waters, and hewed out cisterns for

themselves, broken cisterns that can hold no water." Jer. 2:13

We try to find real joy in relationships, sex, power, authority, fame, accomplishments but we are always thirsty and nothing satisfies us. We are just moving in circles and never reaching what we really desire and are looking for as we are searching in the wrong place. We are simply chasing a mirage. The world promises happiness in material things and people and we run after them only to find out the vanity of it all.

But things are totally different with Jesus, our one and only city of refuge. With Him we are promised that all our shameful past will be removed from us and we will not remember it anymore. All failures, hurts and hard times are going to be replaced. All we need to do is to *completely* surrender to God to wash us from all hurtful memories, heal painful scars and restore everything back to His <u>original</u> plan.
Like a computer that had been infected with viruses, sometimes the only remedy is to allow the manufacturer to reset it to the factory settings.

When you are facing hard times in your journey with God please trust that He will ALWAYS give you joy throughout all of the steps. This joy is not related to what is happening around us but rather with what is happening within.

Remember that Paul and Silas were rejoicing while still in chains inside the prison and long before they were set free. The source of joy came from the presence of the Holy Spirit inside their hearts and not any external factors.

This is one of the fruits of the Holy Spirit and He is the one responsible to fill our hearts with unspeakable joy regardless of all circumstances.

Now being a fugitive in one of the cities of refuge was not the easiest thing or the most pleasant experience you would expect, but it is here that we see God's love for and compassion towards us. Please look at this verse in Job as I believe it summarizes many things.

"You will forget your misery; you will remember it as waters that have passed away." Job 11:16

Allow me to quote two passages here to further explain this verse.

(The water of the river is come by us, and returns no more. The rough, the swollen, the turbid stream, we remember as it foamed and dashed along, threatening to sweep everything away; but it went swiftly by, and will never come back.) Alfred Barnes

(Former afflictions and distresses; having an abundance of prosperity and happiness, and long continued; and so, in process of time, the miseries and distresses before endured are forgotten; thus it was with Joseph in his advanced state, and therefore he called one of his sons Manasseh, and as it is with convinced and converted persons and believers in Christ, who, under first convictions and awakenings, are filled with sorrow and distress, on a view of their miserable estate by nature; but when Christ is revealed to them as their Savior and Redeemer, and the love of God is shed abroad in their hearts, and they have faith and hope in Jesus, and a comfortable view of heaven and happiness, and eternal life, by him, they forget their spiritual poverty, and remember their misery no more, unless it be to magnify the riches of the grace of God) John Gill

Joseph has experienced very hard conditions; betrayed by his brothers and sold to strangers, separated from his father and the whole family, lonely in a pagan land, falsely accused because he refused to disobey God, thrown into prison, forgotten. His life seemed to be shattered down to millions of pieces and anyone could easily feel there is no hope for him.
But then came the abundant blessings.

God made him a blessing to all people of the earth at that time. He **forgot** his captivity and pain and **rejoiced** at last.

Remember that Golan means "their captivity; their rejoicing "
The captivity in Joseph's life and all that it carried from hurts and harsh times have been turned into rejoicing.

God will do the same in your life.
Though you may be passing through the most difficult time of your life, be assured that it will pass by and God will turn things into blessings as long as you are walking in His plan and obeying His voice. As long as you are abiding in Him.

Please note that this does not mean you will never pass in trouble again, it simply means that while troubles may hit again and Satan attacks once more, we will have a new weapon in our hands: Joy.

"for the joy of the LORD is your strength." Neh. 8:10

God's joy is independent upon the surrounding circumstances. It is dependent on who God is and we know that He never changes, He is the same yesterday, today and forever. The Holy Spirit is the one who fills our hearts with such unspeakable joy. We will rejoice after all that has happened to us. God will cause us to forget every hard time and we will just rejoice in Him.

Remember that it is written:
"Then our mouth was filled with laughter, and our tongue with shouts of joy; then they said among the nations, "The LORD has done great things for them." Ps. 126:2

"Weeping may tarry for the night, but joy comes with the morning." Ps. 30:5

Not only this but when the Holy Spirit is living in us, we will be able to rejoice in all

circumstances and in the midst of the hard times even and not just after they pass. When we do this, the enemy is really puzzled and cannot understand how we are having such joy while things appear to be tumbling down around us. This joy is an everlasting one "but I will see you again, and your hearts will rejoice, and no one will take your joy from you." John 16:22
It is here to stay. No one can ever steal this joy from our hearts.
"For the kingdom of God is not a matter of eating and drinking but of righteousness and peace and joy in the Holy Spirit." Rom. 14:7

We were made, as a Church and also as individuals, for such a close and intimate relationship with our Creator and Lover; to receive His abundant love and love Him back. We have the right to enjoy this relationship to the fullest, to receive God's love and rejoice. We are to rejoice every single day of our lives or else we are missing something really big.

"and as the bridegroom rejoices over the bride, so shall your God rejoice over you. " Isa. 62: 5

"rejoice with joy unspeakable and full of glory " 1 Pet. 1:8

Believe me, there is no true joy but in God.

Promises to Manasseh:

The Bible is really a fascinating book. Guess what does Manasseh means?
Manasseh means: "causing to forget"
God will cause you to forget not only troubled times but also all evil things you did, things you are ashamed to speak about. When you come to God and repent and enter into the real city of refuge, He will remove your sins as if they did not exist. Do you remember the Samaritan woman? When she encountered Jesus, she forgot about all her past and was filled with joy to go and tell all the city about Him.
"I have blotted out your transgressions like a cloud and your sins like mist; return to me, for I have redeemed you " Isa. 44:22

He will cause you to forget the sexual abuse you suffered while you were young, the mockery from your friends, the injustice at work, the cheating from your spouse, the shame you felt when you sinned again, the disappointment in yourself after falling in the same sin once more and the list goes on.

Remember this verse again, please:
"You will forget your misery; you will remember it as waters that have passed away."
Job 11:16

Jacob's Promise:

"Joseph is a fruitful bough, a fruitful bough by a spring; his branches run over the wall. The archers bitterly attacked him, shot at him, and harassed him severely, yet his bow remained unmoved; his arms were made agile by the hands of the Mighty One of Jacob, by the God of your father who will help you, by the Almighty who will **bless** you with **blessings** of heaven above, **blessings** of the deep that crouches beneath, **blessings** of the breasts and of the womb. The **blessings** of your father are mighty beyond the **blessings** of my parents, up to the bounties of the *everlasting hills.* May they be on the head of Joseph, and on the brow of him who was set apart from his brothers." Gen. 49: 22-26

Moses' Promise:

"And of Joseph he said, **Blessed** of Jehovah be his land, For the *precious* things of heaven, for the dew, and for the deep that coucheth beneath, and for the *precious* things of the fruits of the sun, and for the *precious* things of the growth of the moons, and for the chief things of the ancient mountains, and for the *precious* things of the *everlasting hills,* and for the *precious* things of the earth and the fulness thereof, and the good will of him that dwelt in the bush. Let *the* **blessing** come upon the head of Joseph, and upon the crown of the head of him that was separate from his brethren. The firstling of his herd, majesty is his; and his horns are the horns of the wild-ox: with them he shall push the peoples all of them, *even* the ends of the earth: and they are the ten thousands of Ephraim, and they are the thousands of Manasseh." Deut. 33: 13-17

Jacob mentioned the trials and attacks that Joseph experienced but he added that despite all of these, his bow remained unmoved and his hands strong by the mighty one of Jacob. The tribulations and hardness will be transformed

into blessings. In the two promises we find
repetition of two words: blessing & precious.

Blessings in the original Hebrew means
prosperity also beside blessings.
That is why we see that Joseph, and hence
Ephraim & Manasseh, will be fruitful and have
the *Precious* things from all around them.
God will grant us abundant blessings and make
us forget years of slavery.
God is the God of restoration.

"I will restore to you the years that the swarming
locust has eaten, the hopper, the destroyer, and
the cutter, my great army, which I sent among
you." Joel 2:25
Also please note that the term "everlasting hills"
occur in the two promises.
This is to indicate that this blessing of joy is an
everlasting one, one that will continue with us in
heaven.
Remember the verse that we already mentioned
"but I will see you again, and your hearts will
rejoice, and no one will take your joy from you."
John 16:22

Chapter 6

Jesus our City of Refuge

Now let us summarize the whole six cities in implication to our nowadays lives, our relationship with Jesus, His redemptive work on the cross and His resurrection.

As we have mentioned earlier before studying each city, the first three are the ones where we are with God and He does inward work in us. He is cleansing us from within, freeing us and shaping our characters after we first fled to Him. In these cities, God is dealing with us internally before using us to proclaim His kingdom. These are the foundation stages. God, being a loving Father, cares so much for our lives even more than our ministry.

This does not mean we need to focus on ourselves and our needs, on the contrary. God promises to take care of all our needs so that we are free to take His message to the whole world and bring His kingdom here on earth.

Also please note that these are not (once-in-a-life-experience). We always need to remain in

Jesus, our city of refuge, and never think we can make it on our own apart from Him. Let me illustrate more so let us take the issue of Holiness for example.

Holiness is not a milestone in our journey with God but rather it is an ongoing daily experience. I cannot say I became totally holy on this specific day. The true essence of holiness is to abide in Jesus each day so that the Holy Spirit always has the freedom to check our hearts, thoughts and actions and cleanse us on our way. "Having therefore these promises, beloved, let us cleanse ourselves from all defilement of flesh and spirit, perfecting holiness in the fear of God." 2 Cor. 7:1

The word used here to describe holiness in our lives is *perfecting.*

Perfecting means to bring to an end, accomplish, perfect, execute, complete. This means that holiness is not a thing we achieve instantly but an ongoing process. We will continue to grow in holiness and all other traits until the day we are with God in heaven.

The other three cities are related to how we live in the world surrounding us and the things God is doing in and through us that are shown to all those around us so that all would give Him glory.

Let us take another look at the cities from this perspective and their meaning as we have shown earlier:

1- Kedesh: Holiness
2- Shechem: Shoulder
3- Hebron: Fellowship
4- Bezer: Strong hold
5- Ramoth: Exaltation
6- Golan: Joy

As we pointed out earlier, we will take the first three together and later the last three together. The first three are related to steps to be taken just between you and God. No other person is in the picture, only you and your loving Father. First thing to notice is that Jesus accepts us as we are. He accepts anyone who cries to Him and returns from his own ways.
The old cities of refuge were open to anyone who fled to them. They were not restricted only to Jews but were open to strangers as well.
This reminds me of one of my favorite worship songs "Blessed be the name of the Lord "
Just look at these words with me:

"Who am I to be part of your people, the ones
that are called by your name, could I be chosen
as one of your own, could it be that our blood is
the same.
*How can a **stranger**, a **remnant** of nations,*
belong to the Royal line?
You showed your grace when the branches were
broken and I grafted into the vine,
Baruch Hashem Adonai,
Baruch Hashem Adonai,
Blessed be the name of the Lord,
Baruch Hashem Adonai.
How could you show me such bountiful mercy by
taking the life of the Lamb,
your love is greater than I can imagine, I bless
you with all that I am.
Praise to you Jesus, the veil has been parted and
what once was secret is known,
now I can cry to you, Abba! my Father! and
praise you as one of your own! "

We were once strangers and remnant of nations
but through Jesus we have been accepted in the
royal family. This is Grace in its clearest and
most marvelous form.
In fact, He is always waiting for us to come back
to Him and to our real home.

Just as the father stood each day waiting for his prodigal son to come home so is God. God will never hide His face from us or accept us with condemnation but on the contrary with open arms of love and mercy.

The veil of the temple was literally torn from top to bottom when Jesus died on the cross to signify that by His death we all have access to God. Jesus became the pure and spotless sacrifice so that we may enter into God's throne by His blood.

"Having therefore, brethren, boldness to enter into the holy place by the blood of Jesus, by the way which he dedicated for us, a new and living way, through the veil, that is to say, his flesh " Heb. 10:19,20

"And, having made peace through the blood of his cross, by him to reconcile all things unto himself; by him, *I say,* whether *they be* things in earth, or things in heaven. And you, that were sometime alienated and enemies in *your* mind by wicked works, yet now hath he reconciled. In the body of his flesh through death, to present you holy and unblameable and unreproveable in his sight " Col. 1: 20-22

Now let us take each city by itself to see how it is applicable to our daily lives.

Kedesh: Holiness

"When I passed by you again and looked upon you, indeed your time was the time of **_love_**; so I spread My wing over you and covered your nakedness. Yes, I swore an oath to you and entered into a **_covenant_** with you, and you became Mine," says the Lord God. " Ezek. 16:8

This is what God does for everyone who comes seeking Him and fleeing sin to abide in the one and true city of refuge. Jesus not only accepts us but He cleanses and sanctifies us and makes us holy like He is.
This is done through His precious blood that was shed on the cross so that we would be holy as He is.

In the above passage, the Lord makes it clear that he yearns for us to come to Him so that we can experience His time of love and enter into a divine covenant with Him. The clear message here is that not only God accepts us, but

moreover He grants us the privilege to be in a
covenant with Him.
What follows then is described in the rest of the
verses so let us take a look at them:

"Then I bathed you with water and washed off
your blood from you and anointed you with oil. I
clothed you also with embroidered cloth and
shod you with fine leather. I wrapped you in
fine linen and covered you with silk. And I
adorned you with ornaments and put bracelets
on your wrists and a chain on your neck.
And I put a ring on your nose and earrings in
your ears and a beautiful crown on your head.
Thus you were adorned with gold and silver, and
your clothing was of fine linen and silk and
embroidered cloth. You ate fine flour and honey
and oil. You grew exceedingly beautiful and
advanced to royalty. And your renown went
forth among the nations because of your beauty,
for it was perfect through the splendor that I had
bestowed on you, declares the Lord God."
Ezek. 16: 9-14

God cleanse us and anoints us with the Holy
Spirit (the use of the words water & oil is a clear
symbol of the Holy Spirit) As we noted earlier,
we cannot do this by ourselves as the sinful

nature within us is always fighting us and pushing us towards sin. Remember that Naphtali, where this city was, means "wrestling". Before coming to God we were always in a state of wrestling with our sinful nature. Let us see how Paul put this idea:

"For I know that nothing good dwells in me, that is, in my flesh. For I have the desire to do what is right, but not the ability to carry it out. For I do not do the good I want, but the evil I do not want is what I keep on doing. Now if I do what I do not want, it is no longer I who do it, but sin that dwells within me. "
Rom. 7:18-20

Here Paul describes a wrestle within himself between two forces.
His desire to do good things as this is the right thing by the law which is yearning deep within us but he finds himself inclined to do evil things. Paul concludes that what forces him to take these wrong choices is the sin that dwells in him. the sinful nature that we inherited and were born with from Adam and Eve when they sinned.
He finally cries out: "wretched man that I am! Who will deliver me from this body of death?"
Rom 7:24

This is the devastated conclusion and it seems there is no hope for him in such situation.

But he does not leave us here but quickly gives the answer.

"There is therefore now no condemnation for those *who are in Christ Jesus*. For the law of the Spirit of life has set you free in Christ Jesus from the law of sin and death. For God has done what the law, weakened by the flesh, could not do. By sending his own Son in the likeness of sinful flesh and for sin, he condemned sin in the flesh" Rom. 8:1-3

You notice that the first verse here speaks about Acceptance and confirms that God will never condemn us but we are always welcomed in the city of refuge.

Paul then continues to shed the light on the only solution for this dilemma that affects all the human race. It is by being in Christ Jesus. Only by God's Spirit can we be set free from this tendency to make evil choices from within.

We need to accept Jesus as king in our lives, surrender to Him and enter into Him as the city of refuge. When we do that, we are united with Him in His death on the cross and resurrection and hence we also die to our sinful nature and are resurrected as a new creation filled with His Spirit.

Let us look at what Jesus did at the last supper with the disciples:

"Jesus, knowing that the Father had given all things into his hands, and that he had come from God and was going back to God, rose from supper. He laid aside his outer garments, and taking a towel, tied it around his waist. Then he poured water into a basin and began to wash the disciples' feet and to wipe them with the towel that was wrapped around him. He came to Simon Peter, who said to him, "Lord, do you wash my feet?" Jesus answered him, "What I am doing you do not understand now, but afterward you will understand." Peter said to him, "You shall never wash my feet." Jesus answered him, "If I do not wash you, you have no share with me." John 13: 3-8

Jesus told Peter that if he doesn't allow Him to wash his feet, he will not have share with Him afterwards. This was a prophetic act as to how Jesus was going to wash away all our sins through His blood. We only need to accept His redemptive work and allow Him to wash us from within.

"Come now, let us reason together, says the LORD: though your sins are like scarlet, they shall be as white as snow; though they are red like crimson, they shall become like wool." Isa. 1: 18

We need to completely surrender to the Holy Spirit and give Him control over our lives as He is the only one capable of transforming our sinful nature to a new one. When we accept Jesus as our lord and savior and accept His redemptive work on the cross and His resurrection, we give Him the right to live in us. We no longer live ourselves but Jesus in us.

After this, God covers our nakedness and uses expensive and beautiful materials so that we may look and feel beautiful as well.
Regardless of how filthy we have been, nothing is impossible for God to fix and restore to its original wonderful design.

Remember that the prodigal son used to sit and eat with pigs but ended with the best robe and a royal ring in his finger. His father accepted him and declared that the day he returned is a day of love. He announced to everyone that he is his son thus retaining the covenant between them and after that, the father took him and gave him new clothes and shoes and a feast was thrown in his honor. " Luke 15: 11-32 "

The same we notice in Ezekiel passage; God then crowns us and gives us
precious jewelry to wear thus confirming our status as His bride and the new Royal nature He bestows on us. We are given fine and delicious food to eat and nurture, the same as the prodigal son had a great feast when he came home.

This is His goal for us: *You grew exceedingly __beautiful__ and advanced to __royalty__.*
This is the true and real relationship that God wants us to be in with Him. This is the way of holiness.

Shechem: Shoulder

After this step, Jesus then removes all our
bondages and chains from us as He already
carried all of these on His shoulders at the cross.
"And it shall come to pass in that day, *that* his
burden shall be taken away from off thy
shoulder, and his yoke from off thy neck, and
the yoke shall be destroyed because of the
anointing." Isa. 10:27
Remember the verse from the book of Ezekiel
that we just looked at, this was one of them:
"and anointed you with oil." Ezek.16:9

We can see here the work of the Holy Spirit
once again in removing every yoke and burden
from our shoulders. The gentle and smooth
anointing of the Spirit will cause these burdens
to dissolve and wear out. And instead of the
burdens that we carried for so long, He makes us
fruitful in an abundant way.
Our backs are straightened once again and we
can finally rest from the heavy burdens that were
on our shoulders.

Jesus wants us to always throw all our worries
and burdens on Him so that we may live the life
He intended for us.

"casting all your anxieties on him, because he cares for you. " 1 Pet. 5:7

We need to carry only His yoke on our shoulders and when we do, Jesus will carry most of its weight with us.

Hebron: Fellowship

We are then called to have fellowship with Him and enter into a deep and intimate relationship with Jesus; our savior and lover.
This is the covenant part in Ezekiel's passage:

"Yes, I swore an oath to you and entered into a ***covenant*** with you, and you became Mine," says the Lord God. " Ezek.16:8

Let us look at these verses from Song of Songs as well as they describe such a relationship that Jesus yearns to be in with each one of us:

"Arise, my darling, my beautiful one, come with me. See! The winter is past; the rains are over and gone. Flowers appear on the earth; the season of singing has come, the cooing of doves is heard in our land. The fig tree forms its early fruit; the blossoming vines spread their fragrance. Arise, come, my darling; my beautiful one, come with me." Song of Songs 2:10 - 13

Once again this reminds me of the lovely book by Hannah Hurnard "Hind's feet on high places "It describes the wonderful transformation that happens in our lives and the intimacy we can experience along the journey with our true lover.

You see, this is one of the main points in our lives with God; to have a real and genuine relationship with Him. God does not want us to worship Him from afar not knowing Him. He does not want us to be sitting under the mountain like the Israelites but to be like Moses over the mountain where there was a true and unique experience and relationship with Him.

Now we move to the next three cities.

As you can notice, God wants us to live His kingdom on earth with all that it has to offer to us and to those around us. Jesus taught His disciples to pray the following: "Your kingdom come, your will be done, on earth as it is in heaven." Matt. 6:10

So what are the things that characterize such a kingdom?

Paul summarizes the traits of such a kingdom as follows:

"For the kingdom of God is not a matter of eating and drinking but of *righteousness* and *peace* and *joy* in the Holy Spirit. " Rom.14:17

Now the kingdom is full of many other characteristics but these three just stand out. We can see these three traits clearly in the last three cities:

Bezer which resembles a Stronghold thus providing us with *peace* even in the midst of all calamities the world is in.

Ramoth which symbolizes Exaltation that is a form of *righteousness* of the kings up high.

Golan which is outstanding, everlasting and out-of-this-world *joy*.

Bezer: Stronghold

God's promise to us is that He will always be a
stronghold and a wall of protection against all
the enemy's attacks
It is written "No weapon that is formed against
thee shall prosper; and every tongue that shall
rise against thee in judgment thou shalt
condemn. This is the heritage of the servants of
Jehovah, and their righteousness which is of me,
saith Jehovah. " Isa. 54:17

No one can ever harm us while we are in His
presence. God is our one and only fortified place
to hide in and feel secure while the whole world
is trembling around us. No enemy or devious
weapon can harm us while we are in the city of
refuge.

I am not referring here to physical protection but
to spiritual one.
Jesus once said: "and fear not them which kill
the body, but are not able to kill the
soul " Matt. 10: 28

Our real battle is not an earthly one but a
spiritual one. Satan wants to destroy and kill
your soul and not the temporary body. The soul

is what will live forever and not that poor physical body.

I believe that this is the protection God is referring to. This is the real and most important protection that our souls will be saved and remain steadfast in Him and not drift away in the middle of the enemy's attack.

This is the only place where we will find true peace.

"And the peace of God, which surpasses all understanding, will guard your hearts and your minds in Christ Jesus." Php 4:7

The word "guard" means to be a watcher in advance, to mount guard as a sentinel. To guard, protect by a military guard, to prevent hostile invasion.

We can find peace of mind from all worries that are haunting the people around us. Worries of securing the future, of being sick, of failing, of being lonely and the list goes on.

Only in Jesus can we find this outstanding peace of mind even in the middle of life's storms. Remember that Jesus was peacefully asleep in the boat in the midst of the storm. God's peace is on all realms, the physical one and most importantly the spiritual one.

But as we already noted, we need to fully depend on Him and surrender all our weapons at the gate of the city. We need to completely trust Him and His power and not take confidence in what we have or know to help us.

"Be sober-minded; be watchful. Your adversary the devil prowls around like a roaring lion, seeking someone to devour." 1 Pet. 5:8
We need to always stay in our city as our enemy is on patrol seeking to destroy anyone who comes out and depends on his own strength or knowledge.

Ramoth: Exaltation

Not only this but we will be exalted to the highest places with Him and be Kings and Priests in the kingdom.
Like what happened to Joseph, we are promised the same. After years of slavery and suffering Joseph was exalted to the highest place in Egypt and ruled over many.
We need to embrace this reality and live accordingly; as kings and priests.

This is our role in the kingdom. We need to embrace this truth and act upon it. We should rule with Jesus and change the reality around us to bring His kingdom here on earth as it is in heaven.

God does not want us to live a life of weakness though the world tries its best to draw this picture regarding those who follow Jesus. They are portrayed as weak and naive and easily deceived but the truth cannot be farther.

Jesus gave us ALL power that was given to Him and ordered us to bring heaven on earth.
We have the right and power to change the reality around us.
We have the right and power to change nations.
We have the right and power to heal the sick and release the captives free from Satan's hand.
We have the right and power to preach the good news and see many come back to God.

Do not be afraid to exercise these rights that you have. Do not be like the slave who buried the talents given to him.
Matt. 25:14-31

So it is high time to fully believe in and realize our role in Jesus and exercise all the authority He has given us to bring His kingdom here on earth.

Golan: Joy

Finally, we are to experience and enjoy overflowing joy all the days of our lives with Him.
Please note that this joy is not just feelings but real deep and genuine joy that you cannot deny and is independent on any circumstances around us but rather coming from the true source of all joy; Jesus.

Even in the middle of trouble and attacks from the enemy, our joy shall prevail and even strengthen us in our journey. We need not fear that someday something would happen and we lose this joy. This everlasting joy has been guaranteed by Jesus himself and no one can ever steal it from our hearts.

We have the right to be joyful each and every day of our journey with Jesus.

Nothing in this world or from the enemy can suppress the divine joy flowing from the Holy Spirit within our hearts.

People will see this joy and wonder how come we got it in the middle of difficult times. This then will be our testimony that it is Jesus who is the true and only source of such joy.

People may even get puzzled and confused and may think we are crazy but the real joy comes from such a close and intimate relationship with Jesus and by just abiding in Him; our city of refuge.

Chapter 7

My Refuge Psalm

Now allow me to spend this chapter meditating on one of the most beautiful psalms, a psalm I would like to call "My Refuge Psalm "

Psalm 91

"He that dwelleth in the secret place of the most High shall abide under the shadow of the Almighty. I will say of the LORD, *He is* my refuge and my fortress: my God; in him will I trust. Surely he shall deliver thee from the snare of the fowler, *and* from the noisome pestilence. He shall cover thee with his feathers, and under his wings shalt thou trust: his truth *shall be thy* shield and buckler. Thou shalt not be afraid for the terror by night; *nor* for the arrow *that* flieth by day; *nor* for the pestilence *that* walketh in darkness; *nor* for the destruction *that* wasteth at noonday.
A thousand shall fall at thy side, and ten thousand at thy right hand; *but* it shall not come

nigh thee. Only with thine eyes shalt thou behold
and see the reward of the wicked.

Because thou hast made the LORD, *which is* my
refuge, *even* the most High, thy habitation;

There shall no evil befall thee, neither shall any
plague come nigh thy dwelling.

For he shall give his angels charge over thee, to
keep thee in all thy ways. They shall bear thee
up in *their* hands, lest thou dash thy foot against
a stone. Thou shalt tread upon the lion and
adder: the young lion and the dragon shalt thou
trample under feet.

Because he hath set his love upon me, therefore
will I deliver him: I will set him on high,
because he hath known my name.

He shall call upon me, and I will answer him: I
will be with him in trouble; I will deliver him,
and honour him. With long life will I satisfy
him, and shew him my salvation. "

I will be studying three different versions of
each verse: King James Version (KJV), The
Passion Translation (TPT) and the Complete
Jewish Bible (CJB) in this order.

Let's take a look at each verse and see how Jesus
is our true and only city of refuge.

1

"He that dwelleth in the secret place of the most High shall abide under the shadow of the Almighty. "

"When you sit enthroned under the shadow of Shaddai, you are hidden in the strength of God Most High. "

"You who live in the shelter of 'Elyon, who spend your nights in the shadow of Shaddai"

The word dwelleth here in its original language means to remain, settle, sit, abide, in quiet. In the Passion translation, the word used is "enthroned" while in the CJB it is "live" We are to settle and live in this place as royalties and kings in their home.
In this place we can settle quietly and find the long searched peace.
This should be our place always, our home. This is where we find rest and strength.
Jesus yearns to be our true home and not someone to go to only when we feel tired or scared or in need. Jesus is calling us to settle in

Him and not only live there and pass our days
but we are to live like Him, as kings.

This word is the key to all this psalm in my
opinion. Whatever follows of promises is tied to
the fact that we remain in this secret place and
dwell in our city of refuge.
If we choose to go out at any time, then we
become exposed to the enemy's attacks just like
any person in the past who went out of the city
of refuge was   exposed to the vengeance of the
killed person's relatives.

One of the best examples to such a principle is
Joshua.
Let us examine what the Bible wrote about him.

"Thus the LORD used to speak to Moses face to
face, as a man speaks to his friend. When Moses
turned again into the camp, his assistant Joshua
the son of Nun, a young man, would not depart
from the tent." Ex. 33:11

You see that Joshua would not depart from the
tent even after Moses has left.
Now Joshua was Moses' assistant so he should
go after him anywhere he goes to help him but
Joshua decided to stay in the place where God

was. This was the place he loved to be. He always put God first in his life, before any other duties.

This is the essence of all this psalm, to dwell and remain in Jesus and never depart from Him.

Now we are all faced daily with many distractions and trials but the key to the blessings in this psalm is summed up in this single word: Dwell, spending our days and nights in this special secret place.

We need to be always connected with the Holy Spirit and giving Him full control over our lives and remain in our city of refuge: Jesus.

Whenever we as a family travel and even when we go to a very nice hotel or resort, nothing competes with our home. Even though our home is a very ordinary one, yet you tend to agree with the saying "There's no place like home "

You can be *free* in your home. You can be *yourself* in your home.

There is a feeling of belonging to this specific place.

The same applies to our spiritual life, we can find this real rest only in our city of refuge: Jesus.

The phrase "Secret place " in this verse serves as a shelter or hiding place thus emphasizing the same idea of security. But there is more here. A secret is normally between two people and they do not speak about it to others. This is something between them that no one else knows about.

A secret is not known or seen or meant to be known or seen by others.

Therefore, secret here simply means that no one else will know this place, only you and God.

Can you imagine that God promises to hide you and keep you safe in a place not known to anyone else; not to angels, humans and definitely not to demons.

The devil will not be able to reach me as he does not even know where I am.

So in this place there is maximum and absolute safety. As long as I stay in the city of refuge, each day I have this right to be in this special place.

Look at these verses that confirm the same reality.

"For in the time of trouble he shall hide me in his pavilion: in the *secret* of his tabernacle shall he hide me; he shall set me up upon a rock. " Ps. 27:5

"Thou shalt hide them in the *secret* of thy presence from the pride of man: thou shalt keep them *secretly* in a pavilion from the strife of tongues." Ps. 31:20

Remember that it is written "for he who touches you touches the apple of his eye" Zech. 2:8

"Most High" here is the Hebrew word "Elyon" as it is written in the CJB. This is a name of God in the Old Testament that means that He is the one higher than any other gods or people. So this secret place belongs to the Most High God. Just imagine who can enter into such a place if he has not already been given access to. Moreover, who can know such a place from the beginning and even if it is known, who can go there?

"Abide": The same idea is further hammered using the word abide. Abide means to remain all night as it is in the CJB.

In the Passion Translation the word used is "hidden" thus confirming the idea of the secret place where no one can reach us and we are hidden from the face and knowledge of our enemy. It is also the same Hebrew word used for an eagle passing the night on the high cliffs.

In night we mainly allow our bodies to rest. Also, it is safe to be inside your home at night to be protected from any dangers roaming in the darkness.

Night is often associated with fear and unknown terrors but in God we can stay assured and secure. Only in God can we find real and perfect rest and safety.

"under the shadow of the Almighty "
The psalmist used the word shadow for a specific reason, nothing is used haphazard in the Bible but every word is from God.

To use such a word means that I am really close to God that His shadow will be upon me.

Imagine being that close to the Almighty God of the whole universe and walking beside Him.

To be in someone's shadow means He is taking everything before me; the heat of the sun, the wind, the rain, so that I am only in the shadow. I am hidden behind Him.

When I am with my son on a hot and sunny day (which is the normal in Egypt), I always try to adjust my position so that I am between him and the blazing rays of the sun. He is therefore in my shadow, protected from the heat and moreover enjoying a cool place. In order for this to happen I need to be very close to him and moreover, he needs to stay close to me as well.

If he decided to move away on his own, he will depart from my shadow and be exposed to the sun.
The same happens in our relationship with God. If we decided to go on our own ways and leave the city of refuge, we are then totally exposed to all of the enemy's weapons against us.
We are the ones who choose to step away from the divine protection. God never leaves us, it is we who walk away. We are the ones who choose to get out of the city but the city never decides to move away.

We are in the shadow of the Almighty, "Shaddai", the mighty one.

He is so strong that we are completely secure and safe in Him. No one can harm us or do anything as long as we are in Him. The same case if we are in the city of refuge, no avenger can harm us or demand our blood.

So imagine you are in the shadow of El Shaddai, the Almighty One.

2

"I will say of the LORD, *He is* my refuge and
my fortress: my God; in him will I trust"

"He's the hope that holds me, and the
Stronghold to shelter me, the only God for me,
and my great Confidence "

"who say to ADONAI, "My refuge! My fortress!
My God, in whom I trust!"

"Lord" here in the Hebrew is Jehovah which
means I am; the eternal living one.
The name Jehovah shows God's nature as He
stands in relation to man, as the only almighty,
true, personal, holy being.
As for Adonai, Hawker states the following:

"This is one of the names peculiarly applied to
the person of the Lord Jesus Christ. It is a sweet
and interesting name of the Lord Jesus. It carries
with it the idea of a stay, or helper, security,
confidence. "

So Adonai here refers to Jesus as my only city of
refuge.

Please note that "my " was repeated three times in this single verse. Even in the Passion translation we find three "me " and " my " also while in the CJB, it is repeated three times as well. This is to emphasize the importance of this truth; He is My refuge and fortress.

He is A PERSONAL GOD and not a far and away one.

This is very personal and not a general relationship. We may be sometimes satisfied with just attending church and serving in various meetings, paying our tithes and doing our community obligations but God is calling each one into a deeper and intimate relationship with Him.

We have this privilege through the work of Jesus to abide in the one and true city of refuge.

God is the almighty, the true one and my God.

The psalmist uses here the Hebrew word Elohim (God)

This is the plural form and is used to describe God the Father, Jesus the Son and the Holy Spirit.

We are called to have a relationship with God the Father; He is my heavenly father, the one who knew me before I was even formed.

"Your eyes saw my unformed substance; in your book were written, every one of them, the days that were formed for me, when as yet there was none of them. " Ps. 139:16
He is the father that sent His only son to die in my place.

We are called also to have a relationship with Jesus; our savior, redeemer, friend and elder brother. Imagine Jesus as your best friend, what could your day be like? This is exactly what Jesus said: "but I have called you friends. "John 15:15

Also we are called into the same relationship with the Holy Spirit; our counselor, teacher and companion in our daily walks.

Trust here means also to be bold and secure, as well as confident in what was spoken.
"Now faith is the assurance of things hoped for, the conviction of things not seen. "
Heb. 11:1

Jesus is our hope and confidence. We do not hope in things or people or circumstances. We do not place our hope in money, relationships or positions.

We hope in Jesus himself and it is Jesus that holds us and encourages us throughout our journey.

Let us then not trust in anything or anyone else except God.

Not in our abilities, money, power, knowledge, experience, people, relations, friends, success….. Only in Him.

3

"Surely he shall deliver thee from the snare of the fowler, *and* from the noisome pestilence. "

"He will rescue you from every hidden trap of the enemy, and he will protect you from false accusation and any deadly curse "

"he will rescue you from the trap of the hunter and from the plague of calamities "

Surely signifies doubtlessness. I am confident in this and there is not even any chance of not happening. What God promises to us will come to pass.

Paul expressed this truth in a clear way "fully convinced that God was able to do what he had promised." Rom. 4:21
I always teach my children to trust what I promise them to do. The same applies with our heavenly father. We need to trust what He promises to do and expect it whatever the surroundings are. God does not exaggerate or give false promises. He is not a man to lie but He is *always faithful.*

This is related to the previous verse where we found that Jesus is our hope and so we have this full assurance that He will deliver and save us.

Deliver here means to snatch away or rescue as it is used in the other two versions.

Imagine that one of your children is crossing the road and you see a speedy car coming from the distance and calculate that it will hit your child, what will your reaction be? You will act quickly to run and snatch him from the road and even push him to safety. You will not explain ahead what you will be doing as there is no time to do so.

Sometimes God interferes in an unexpected way for our own safety.

He may even allow strange things to happen in our lives and we may be puzzled, confused and even not comfortable with these, but we need to have complete confidence that He does everything for our own safety and benefit. He is our loving father.

"And we know that for those who love God all things work together for good, for those who are called according to his purpose." Rom. 8:28

God is our loving father. He is not like any earthly father regardless of how good or not your earthly dad is, God is totally different.

He will act swiftly to rescue you as you are His most precious son or daughter.

As long as we abide in our city of refuge, we will always enjoy this divine protection.

"There is none like God, O Jeshurun, who rides through the heavens to your help, through the skies in his majesty."

Deut. 33:26

Whom does God save us from? He saves us from the Fowler, the Enemy and the Hunter.

Fowler means trapper, bait-layer or hunter. This enemy lies in ambush and sets his snares and traps so that if we go out of the city of refuge he might catch us.

These are hidden snares that may look normal and innocent from outside but once we step on them, they trap our legs and we cannot get out.

The enemy uses many baits to lure us out of our refuge so let's take a look at some of his popular ones:

Sexual temptations:

This may involve entering into a physical relation or even watching certain movies, websites or magazines. This may also include movies that are not porn but have some scenes that the devil can and will use to trap us. The devil will find many excuses for such traps:

- It is just friendship: First of all, there is nothing wrong in friendship in its proper meaning but the devil is using the terminology and twisting it. We need to examine this from two perspectives. For a single person, having friends from the other gender is a healthy thing but if one person is getting closer than all the others, always thinking of this person and the relationship is starting to get physical, you need to be on the alert. The physical part will start slowly but will accelerate rapidly. For a married person, the devil may use marital problems to let you get attracted to another person. Please be aware of such schemes.

- This is part of the movie so you cannot skip it: Well I am a huge movies fan but still I cannot tolerate such an idea. Media has a special influence and what you see, the devil will use it

and keep reminding you of it. You will lose nothing if you skip this scene or even this whole movie. Better be safe than sorry. Remember it is written: "give no opportunity to the devil."
Eph. 4:27

- These pictures will not harm you, after all they are only pictures: No they are not. The persons who are contributing in the porn industry are influenced by the devil and by watching such sites or magazines, you are giving access to the devil to your heart.

Please see what the Bible spoke about the sexual sins as "For she hath cast down many wounded: yea, many strong *men* have been slain by her "
Prov. 7:26

Traps in work:

We may be tempted to act unethically to defend ourselves or to reach certain goals. Are we going to bend our standards? These are some examples the enemy often uses in the work place:

- It is only a white lie: Nothing is called white, grey, blue or any other color lie, a lie is a lie.

These is also nothing called a big lie or small one, these are all fable trials from the world to justify our wrong doing.

- You don't need to say the whole truth, only a part will be enough. Maybe hiding part of the truth will help you progress in certain ways or avoid consequences of special actions that were not right, but would Jesus who is living inside of me say part of the truth and hide another? I highly doubt that, even if this leads to unfavorable reactions.
Remember Maradona, the Argentinian football team captain at the World Cup 1986, in the famous match against England. He scored a goal by his hand but he never confessed it. He rather joked saying it was the hand of God. Imagine if he went to the referee and said the whole truth, the goal would have been disallowed and Argentina might have lost this match which was their way to reach the final and win the whole tournament. He might have lost the most prestigious award in the football world but he would have gained the applause of Heaven instead and the respect of millions.

- You should not help others as they may get ahead of you: This is totally against what the

Bible teaches us regarding love. This is not how the kingdom of God works. We need to love all who are around us, even our enemies, and reflect God's love to them. If you only care about yourself, you may reach very high positions but you will be less like Jesus and more like the world.

Pride:

The devil fell because of pride and he can destroy us by playing on this note. Are we proud enough so as not to apologize, not to acknowledge our weaknesses, not to forgive?

- He will say this is not pride, it is just dignity: Let us first define the word "pride "
  Pride means: the quality of having an excessively high opinion of oneself or one's importance, a person or thing that is the object or source of a feeling or deep pleasure or satisfaction.

When the only thing that matters is your own image and you are focusing only on yourself, that is pride.

Remember that this was the first recorded sin: "How you are fallen from heaven, O Day Star, son of Dawn! How you are cut down to the ground, you who laid the nations low! You said in your heart, 'I will ascend to heaven; above the stars of God I will set my throne on high; I will sit on the mount of assembly in the far reaches of the north " Isa. 14: 12,13

"You were in Eden, the garden of God; every precious stone was your covering, sardius, topaz, and diamond, beryl, onyx, and jasper, sapphire, emerald, and carbuncle; and crafted in gold were your settings and your engravings. On the day that you were created they were prepared.

You were an anointed guardian cherub. I placed you; you were on the holy mountain of God; in the midst of the stones of fire you walked. You were blameless in your ways from the day you were created, till unrighteousness was found in you. In the abundance of your trade you were filled with violence in your midst, and you sinned; so I cast you as a profane thing from the mountain of God, and I destroyed you, O guardian cherub, from the midst of the stones of fire. Your heart was proud because of your beauty; you corrupted your wisdom for the sake of your splendor. I cast you to the ground; I exposed you before kings, to feast their eyes on you." Ezek. 28:13-17

Lucifer was so consumed by his own beauty that he became so proud. This was the main thing that led to his fall. Beware of the different terminologies that Satan would describe your actions with so as to justify them.

"Pride goes before destruction, and a haughty spirit before a fall." Prov.16:18

- All other people are acting the same way so you should act similarly: Well this is the main reason to not do so. We are called to be different than other people and to reflect Jesus in all our ways.
"You are the salt of the earth, but if salt has lost its taste, how shall its saltiness be restored? It is no longer good for anything except to be thrown out and trampled under people's feet. You are the light of the world. A city set on a hill cannot be hidden " Matt. 5:13,14

Remember that if we abide in our city of refuge, God Himself will rescue us.

"He delivered me from my strong enemy, and from them which hated me: for they were too strong for me. " Ps. 18:17

"Our soul is escaped as a bird out of the snare of the fowlers: the snare is broken, and we are escaped. " Ps. 124:7

Pestilence here means plague. In the Passion translation it is described as a deadly curse while in the CJB it is describes as plague of calamities.

This is a hidden enemy. You cannot see him coming but only see his effects. This is something that is hitting and affecting all who are around us and causing much disaster. Maybe fear from certain events that are happening, generational curses affecting our lives, whole communities acting in an ungodly way.

I remember when the revolution took place in our country, all the people spent days and weeks in complete ambiguity. There was a spirit of fear all around us; fear of criminals set loose after most prisons were broken, fear of a fallen economy, fear of religious discrimination. Also there was a spirit of aggressiveness and cruelty all around, as if no one cares about any laws anymore and cannot tolerate any other person.

You could easily get swallowed by these deadly spirits and take a spiral downfall giving the devil room in your heart and mind to fill with his lies and fears thus leading you away from God and trying to take things into your own hands to control them.

There are many "plagues" that can affect whole areas or communities as well.

These can affect churches too. You can find a church with all its members very proud of themselves and their church that they look down to other churches or denominations and cannot accept any sort of correction.

Or you may find other churches shutting off the work of the Holy Spirit totally and not giving Him any place or freedom in their lives.

These plagues are so deadly and have a desire to destroy you.

Moreover, they will act like a curse on coming generations until these are divinely exposed and broken by the power of the blood of the lamb. Some may say curses do not exist in the first place so let us examine the Bible and see what it teaches us then.

When king David killed Uriah and took his wife after he had already committed adultery with her, Nathan the prophet came to him with these words:

"Now therefore the sword shall never depart from your house, because you have despised me and have taken the wife of Uriah the Hittite to be your wife." 2 Sam. 12:10

You could easily see this coming in place with all the killings that happened between David's descendants.

Also these plagues are sneaky ones so they are associated with darkness and night (see verse 6) Only God can deliver us from such deadly and sneaky attacks and curses.

We must remain in Him and give Him full authority over our lives.

I like this part a lot from The Treasury of David:

"He who is a Spirit can protect us from evil spirits, he who is mysterious can rescue us from mysterious dangers, he who is immortal can redeem us from mortal sickness. There is a deadly pestilence of error, we are safe from that if we dwell in communion with the God of truth; there is a fatal pestilence of sin, we shall not be

infected by it if we abide with the Holy One. "
(Treasury of David)

Even if what we are facing is confusing to us
and we cannot fully comprehend it, God is the
only one capable of rescuing us from such
attacks. Nothing is too hard for Him.

The key is to abide in our Hope, our City of
Refuge: Jesus.

4

"He shall cover thee with his feathers, and under his wings shalt thou trust: his truth *shall be thy* shield and buckler. "

"His massive arms are wrapped around you, protecting you. You can run under his covering of majesty and hide. His arms of faithfulness are a shield keeping you from harm. "

"he will cover you with his pinions, and under his wings you will find refuge; his truth is a shield and protection. "

Pinions here means the outer part of a bird's wing including the flight feathers.
Now the word feathers used here in the original Hebrew is a feminine noun. As if the verse is speaking about the female bird's feathers.

I suggest that this bird here is an eagle. I am assuming this mainly because of this verse: "As an eagle stirreth up her nest, fluttereth over her young, spreadeth abroad her wings, taketh them, beareth them on her wings " Deut. 32:11

Here also it is referred to as the female eagle
"her "
I searched for eagles on the Internet and this is
part of what I discovered:

"In the eagle family the female eagle is bigger
and stronger than the male.
Feathers are thought to be stronger than any
wing structure made by man and yet at the same
time incredibly flexible so that on the down
stroke of flight they can bend on occasion,
almost at a right angle to allow both lift and
forward movement.
Bald eagles have 7,000 feathers. Feathers consist
of interlocking microscopic structures that are
light, but very strong. Layers of feathers trap air
to insulate birds against cold and protect them
from rain. "

As if God is telling us that He will cover us with
strong and big wings and under these wings and
feathers we are completely protected and
secured from whatever the enemy attacks us
with.
These wings are majestic ones with royal power
thus offering complete and perfect protection. In
the Passion translation, this idea is described as

being under God's massive arms, completely wrapped by them and perfectly protected.

Like a father who takes his child into his bosom and wraps his hands around him.
Such a child will only feel safe and loved regardless of what is going around him so just imagine you being in such a position with your heavenly loving Father.
There is no other place of safety and security I could dream or think about other than this.

We are promised with divine and perfect protection but this protection is not a rigid one that we feel trapped or imprisoned by it. On the contrary, such a protection gives us the ultimate freedom and flexibility in our lives.
God is a good god and He always wants what is best for us. He does not want us to just hide but He cares much about our growth and progress.

Remember when king Saul gave David his armor. David felt very uncomfortable and as if he could not move freely. Saul's intentions were good but the execution was not.
It is similar to parents overprotecting their kids. They care and love them but they can harm them with this unhealthy overprotection.

God here uses the feathers to teach us a valuable concept. His protection is the strongest ever yet He gives us flexibility to be ourselves.

The word "trust" in this verse means also to seek refuge or flee for refuge.
We need to run into Jesus and enter into our city of refuge believing for sure that we have security there.

"His truth "refers to His word (Jesus) and all that God promises for you.
This truth is your safety against all the devil's attacks and lies.
God's word is a mighty weapon in our hands and we need to know how to use it as Jesus did with the devil in the desert. When Satan came to tempt Jesus, Jesus used verses from the Old Testament as the ultimate weapon against the devil so that is a really good reason we should be very close to the word of God to be able to use this weapon when needed.
The spoken word of God scares the devil and causes him to flee from us.
God's words are very powerful and always accomplish what they mean.

Any king has power and he expresses this power in words. He only needs to say what he wants to be done and those who work for him will carry his words to fulfillment. His power is measured by the degree of effectiveness that what he says comes to happen in the actual world.

But still, earthly kings are confined to the limits of power that they have. They cannot order anything unless it is within their power.

Also any king may be faced with circumstances that hinder the completion of what he wants. Even if he had the power, there may be another more powerful king who is opposing him thus preventing his words to become reality.

Our heavenly father is the true king of kings and His power has no limits.

Whatever He says will come to pass for sure in His time. He is never late but precisely on the perfect time.

"so shall my word be that goes out from my mouth; it shall not return to me empty, but it shall accomplish that which I purpose, and shall succeed in the thing for which I sent it." Isa. 55:11

Moreover, there is no one who can stand in front of Him or His will. Nothing in heaven or on earth can oppose His will or delay His timings. So, whatever you have heard from God, whether it was yesterday or years ago, hold strong to it, wait in faith and it shall come to pass.

All what we need to do is stick to His words, save them in your hearts, believe that what He promised He is able to accomplish and wait for it to come.

We put our faith in Jesus Himself who is quite capable of fulfilling all His words and promises.

Now we come to a very strange word that has been used only in this verse in the whole Bible; buckler.

According to Alfred Barnes: "The word rendered "buckler" is derived from the verb "to surround," and is given to the defensive armor here referred to, because it "surrounds," and thus "protects" a person."
(Alfred Barnes)

It also means "coat of mail "which is a jacket covered with or composed of metal rings or plates, serving as armor.

This means there is a double armor.

God's powerful wings and arms are surrounding us in a way that we are completely secure. When we are rooted in it, God's word encompasses us as an armor. It is our shield against all the devil's weapons. We need to hold on to His word and promises in the face of any trials or temptations from our enemy.

Faith in God's word is our shield "In all circumstances take up the shield of faith, with which you can extinguish all the flaming darts of the evil one " Eph. 6:16
And also His word is used as an offensive weapon "and take the helmet of salvation, and the sword of the Spirit, which is the word of God " Eph. 6:17
So let us keep His word very close to us and hide it in our hearts.
"Thy word have I hid in mine heart, that I might not sin against thee. " Ps. 119:11

5,6

"Thou shalt not be afraid for the terror by night; *nor* for the arrow *that* flieth by day. *Nor* for the pestilence *that* walketh in darkness; *nor* for the destruction *that* wasteth at noonday."

"You will never worry about an attack of demonic forces at night nor have to fear a spirit of darkness coming against you. Don't fear a thing! Whether by night or by day, demonic danger will not trouble you, nor will the powers of evil launched against you. For God will keep you safe and secure; they won't lay a hand on you. "

"You will not fear the terrors of night or the arrow that flies by day, or the plague that roams in the dark, or the scourge that wreaks havoc at noon. "

I am sure that most of you are familiar with the term 24/7
It simply means that this place for example is open the whole day and you can drop by or call any time and you will get the service you are asking for.

This is exactly the same concept being used here; God is promising those who dwell in Him a 24/7 protection. It doesn't matter what time of the day or where we are, this protection is there to stay as long as we remain in our city of refuge.

The usage of night and day in these two verses signifies protection against all known and unknown weapons and schemes of the enemy against us.
It also draws a picture of a complete protection, round the clock, whether we are aware of it or not, awake or asleep.
Moreover, we even don't need to worry about it as God promises to be in control and protect us.

Now we come to examine the types and nature of the weapons used by our enemy. These weapons might be some sort of fear and terror that robs us our peace and dependence on God and drive us to worry and depend on ourselves in order to solve the situation or problem.
Or they might be some sort of painful accidents, physically or spiritually, that attack our faith and trust in God.

There are many kinds of attacks but let's focus

on what these verses talk about. We will examine four different types, first two are personal, second two are public:

- Terror / Demonic Forces: Fear
- Arrow / Spirit of darkness: Painful accidents, physical or spiritual.
- Pestilence / Plague: (community attacks) that is hitting all who are around us.
- Destruction / Scourge / powers of evil: Physical attacks.

Please note that Terror & Plague are associated with night and darkness due to their creepy nature and sneaky penetration. They sneak around and penetrate without us even knowing or sensing their coming. There is no warning. It is mentioned that it walketh in darkness. Walketh here means stalks, to pursue or approach a prey. The devil is monitoring us and waiting for the right time to attack and this right time is when we are out of the city of refuge; out of the relationship with God.

"Be sober-minded; be watchful. Your adversary the devil prowls around like a roaring lion, seeking someone to devour "1 Pet. 5:8

On the other hand, Arrows and Destructions are associated with the day and light. This is so that to be able to see the gruesomeness and awfulness of such calamities and accidents so as to add to their horrible effect on us and to instill fear in our hearts.

Our world is ruled by fear and this fear has a strong power.

We are surrounded with fear; fear of failure, fear of being lonely, fear of getting poor, fear over our health, fear over our families and loved ones, fear from things we have no control over, fear from natural disasters, fear from people and the list goes on.

Fear paralyses us and make us unable to think or act properly. Moreover, it leads us to depend on our own strength and knowledge rather that God. Fear is one of the traits of Satan's kingdom.

On the contrary, love is the flagship trait of our heavenly Father's kingdom.

"There is no fear in love; but perfect love casteth out fear: because fear hath torment. He that feareth is not made perfect in love. "
1 John 4:18

Our main and strongest weapon against all fears

from the devil is love.

When we are rooted in God's love and enjoying it, this love will cast away all our fears. We need this love to be very deep in our lives so it can stand against all fears that the enemy throws at us.

Like a plant with its roots running deep and fixed to the ground so that no matter how strong winds are blowing, this plant will never be shaken.

"so that Christ may dwell in your hearts through faith that you, being rooted and grounded in love, "Eph. 3:17

Just imagine that you are the son/daughter of the most powerful king of the most powerful kingdom that has ever been, whom would you fear?

Jesus conquered everything including death so what should we be afraid of?

We covered the community attacks before so I want to give time to the physical incidents now, whether personal or nature destruction.

The question that jumps right away is: why does

God sometimes allow one of his children to have cancer? Why does God allow such a terrible disaster like a tsunami, hurricanes or Covid-19 to occur thus killing thousands of people, including some who believe in Him? Aren't those supposed to be under the complete protection of the city of refuge?
What about what happened to Job? Where was the divine protection?

These are all very legitimate questions and let us ponder a while here trying to find answers.
In my opinion, the best place to find answers for such hard questions is the Bible.

First let's remember that this earth is ruled by the devil.
Adam and Eve were first given authority over all the earth and everything on it.

"And God blessed them. And God said to them, "Be fruitful and multiply and fill the earth and subdue it, and have dominion over the fish of the sea and over the birds of the heavens and over every living thing that moves on the earth."
Gen. 1:28

After that when Adam and Eve first sinned, they

handed this authority over this planet to the devil so he is in control now. The power that was given to Adam and Eve to rule over all the earth was handed over to Satan by the fall of mankind.

But not FULL control.
Let's examine this verse:

"I will no longer talk much with you, for the ruler of this world is coming. He has no claim on me" John 14:30

Now Jesus himself said that Satan is the ruler of this world and thus he has power but the verse does not stop here. There is good news following.
Satan has no claim on Jesus. He has not even one thing on Him.
Jesus came on earth as a man and Satan could not find sin in Him. He was the only solution to our eternal problem. He was the only person on earth that Satan had no control over as sin was not to be found in Him.
We are all born with sin inside of us due to Adam and Eve's transgression but not Jesus.

"knowing that you were ransomed from the futile ways inherited from your forefathers, not with perishable things such as silver or gold, but with the precious blood of Christ, like that of a lamb without blemish or spot." 1 Pet. 1:18,19

Jesus was the perfect lamb without any sin. Not only this but Jesus defeated the devil by His death and resurrection. By doing this, all of us who abide in Jesus are under God's protection.

"We know that everyone who has been born of God does not keep on sinning, but he who was born of God protects him, and the evil one does not touch him. We know that we are from God, and the whole world lies in the power of the evil one." 1 John 5: 18,19

Satan cannot harm us without God's knowledge but does this mean that God allow him to harm us? Is this what happened to Job?
That would be so harsh really and I would not want to follow such a god.
I do not believe this is the case.

I believe that God is in control over the lives of those who follow Him. When we choose to follow God with all our hearts and surrender to His will in our lives, we are united with Him in His death and resurrection and thus are no longer under the power of the ruler of this world but we are subject of the kingdom of heaven.

We are now members of that kingdom and hence we are no longer members of the earth. This leads automatically to the fact that the ruler of this world, Satan, will have nothing on us.

God knows the best for us and all who surround us. Remember that ALL things work to the good of those who love Him.

"And we know that for those who love God all things work together for good, for those who are called according to his purpose." Rom. 8:28

When Satan comes to tempt us, God is not surprised. God actually knows every step that the devil will take. The devil is a created being and God is the one who created him so God knows all that is in his mind and his next move.

God will allow some trials to affect us for our own good.

Job suffered a lot but all was for his own good. He did not see this at first and even did not get all the answers he asked for but the most important thing is that he knew God and his character was shaped in a different way.

But another question appears here:
Could not God use another simpler method?
Were all the pain and loss really necessary?
That was one of Job's questions for sure and he
never got an answer to it.
Instead he was challenged by God to trust in His
wisdom and judgment. To trust that He was in
full control.

Sometimes we might not understand everything
surrounding us but it may all come to the simple
point of belief.
Do we believe in God? Do we believe that He
loves us a never-ending love and that everything
will work out for our good as long as we abide
in Him?
If so then we sometimes need to just focus on
Him and have faith in Him.

The devil has power in the earthly realm and he
is using it in a harsh way, but God is way
stronger that He uses these attacks and turns
them to our benefits.

Remember what Joseph told his brothers after
they were reunited once more:
"As for you, you meant evil against me, but God
meant it for good, to bring it about that many

people should be kept alive, as they are today."
Gen. 50:20

So God knows every step that the devil will take and God even interferes sometimes and restrains the devil from certain attacks as He did with Job.

"And the LORD said to Satan, "Behold, all that he has is in your hand. Only against him do not stretch out your hand." So Satan went out from the presence of the LORD." Job 1:12

"And the LORD said to Satan, "Behold, he is in your hand; only spare his life." Job 2:6

Next time when you face hard times and trials, please do not doubt God's love and protection but have a simple child's faith in Him.
He is in control.

Another point to ponder upon here is the nature of the whole battle we are living in. The battle that our enemy wages against us seems more physical by its nature; accidents, diseases, wars, famines….. but his real aim is our spirits.

In the wonderful book "The Fourth Dimension " by David Yonggi Cho, he sheds the light on the dimension we often neglect in our lives, the spiritual realm.

We are living spirits. Our bodies will fail someday and decompose and cease to exist but our spirits will be there for ever.

Let's examine these verses:
"And do not fear those who kill the body but cannot kill the soul. Rather fear him who can destroy both soul and body in hell." Matt. 10:28

Here soul means spirit. Jesus is warning regarding our spirits and not our flesh.

What Satan desires the most is not just to infect us with a disease or to cause pain but to destroy our spirits and have as many spirits separated from God as possible and dragged with him to hell forever.

When I was sick with Covid-19 and had to be hospitalized, I had to stay there for 24 days all alone. Not seeing my wife, kids, family or friends. These were extremely hard times, not only physically but it was even harder on my soul. Sometimes I could not even pray and many times I was about to give up everything and lose myself in disappointment and shame but I

decided to trust God even though I had little
faith but God strengthened me and He kept my
soul safe during this hard time. The real battle in
my opinion was the spiritual one, whether I will
lose all hope or still hold on to God. God did
heal me physically in a miraculous way but for
me the greater miracle was preserving my soul
from giving up. He sustained me through the
delayed time.

"How we handle God's ordained delays is a
good measure of our spiritual maturity. If we
allow such delays to make us drift off into sin or
lapse into resignation to fate, then we react
poorly to His ordained delays. If we allow such
times to deepen our perseverance in following
God, then they are of good use."
David Guzik

"For we do not wrestle against flesh and blood,
but against the rulers, against the authorities,
against the cosmic powers over this present
darkness, against the spiritual forces of evil in
the heavenly places." Eph. 6:12
Here is another clear verse to the type and nature
of the war we are facing daily.
So let's always be aware that we are living in
this spiritual dimension.

7,8

"A thousand shall fall at thy side, and ten thousand at thy right hand; *but* it shall not come nigh thee. Only with thine eyes shalt thou behold and see the reward of the wicked. "

"Even in a time of disaster with thousands and thousands being killed, you will remain unscathed and unharmed. You will be a spectator as the wicked perish in judgment, for they will be paid back for what they have done "

"A thousand may fall at your side, ten thousand at your right hand; but it won't come near you. Only keep your eyes open, and you will see how the wicked are punished. "

The use of thousand here is to denote the number itself and as a symbol for a company of men under one leader or some troops.

Fall in this verse also means fail.
Even though many fall beside me and very close but nothing will harm me or come near me. Remember that you are hidden in God's secret place and no one can reach you there. Again I

am speaking mainly about your soul which is the
most precious thing and not the body.

The real battle is around the soul and not the
body.

Let's examine the story of the last plague on
Egypt, the death of the first born.

"For I will pass through the land of Egypt this
night, and will smite all the firstborn in the land
of Egypt, both man and beast; and against all the
gods of Egypt I will execute judgment: I *am* the
LORD. And the blood shall be to you for a token
upon the houses where ye *are:* and when I see
the blood, I will pass over you, and the plague
shall not be upon you to destroy *you,* when I
smite the land of Egypt. "Ex.12:12,13

The Israelites were divinely protected against the
loss of their firstborn by the blood upon their
homes. This was a judgment from God but if any
Israeli was out of his blood-marked home, then
this judgment would have fallen on him as well.
All around them they could hear screaming and
crying for many deaths, thousands were falling
beside them but no harm was upon them at all.

There is a promise of a divine protection against

all the enemy's attacks. Though the attacks are everywhere and affecting thousands yet they will never be close to the one who abides in Jesus. These attacks are of the same nature that we discussed earlier so this promise of protection is covering all different types of spiritual, emotional and physical attacks.

Moreover, for him who makes the Most High his shelter, he will watch the punishment of the wicked. This is all what shall happen to him who abides in Jesus and makes the Almighty his refuge. He will be just a spectator.

"Only - That is, this is "all" that will occur to you. The only thing which you have to anticipate is, that you will see how God punishes sinners. "(Albert Barnes)

Even in the CJB version, it is being urged that we keep our eyes open to see the end of those who did not choose the city of refuge.
We all have a solemn duty and a divine call to point the people around us towards the true city of refuge so as they escape the vengeance of the enemy and the reward of the wicked.

9,10

"Because thou hast made the LORD, *which is* my refuge, *even* the most High, thy habitation; There shall no evil befall thee, neither shall any plague come nigh thy dwelling. "

"When we live our lives within the shadow of the God Most High, our secret Hiding place, we will always be shielded from harm! How then could evil prevail against us, or disease infect us? "

"For you have made ADONAI, the Most High, who is my refuge, your dwelling-place. No disaster will happen to you, no calamity will come near your tent"

Habitation in the dictionary means "the state or process of living in a particular place" This refers to a place that is your home and not just a temporarily place. This should be a place of dwelling and not just visiting on certain occasions.

We don't go to Jesus just in the time of need or danger, but we ought to make this city of refuge our permanent address, the place we abide and live in daily, our home.

Habitation also refers to the Tabernacle or the Temple. It refers to the place were we live in connection with our God. The Tabernacle and later the temple were the houses of the Lord in the Old Testament and the presence of God was there.
Joshua always stayed at the entrance of the Tabernacle. He chose the nearest point where he can stay beside the presence of God.
"And the LORD spake unto Moses face to face, as a man speaketh unto his friend. And he turned again into the camp: but his servant Joshua, the son of Nun, a young man, departed not out of the tabernacle." Ex. 33:11

"For a day in thy courts *is* better than a thousand. I had rather be a doorkeeper in the house of my God, than to dwell in the tents of wickedness." Ps 84:10

This should nowadays go further than a physical place and into a spiritual one. We are not called now to spend our entire lives inside a church building but rather in Jesus Himself who lives in us.
Paul said it clearly: "Do you not know that you

are God's temple and that God's Spirit dwells in you?" 1 Cor. 3:16
Jesus is our habitation and this home is a secret hiding place where we will be always protected and divinely covered. We are called to live such a life, a life filled with the Holy Spirit and totally submitted to Him.

The word evil here has been used in the Bible with several meanings. Here are some of these meanings along with how many times each was mentioned in the Bible: evil (440), wickedness (59), hurt (20), mischief (19), bad (14), sore (9), trouble (9) ill (8), affliction (5), harm (5), adversity (3), grievous (2), mischiefs (2), naught (2), noisome (2), wickedly (2)
This is to confirm to us that there is a *complete* protection against any kind of evil attack or scheme from the enemy as long as we are inside the city of refuge;
Jesus Christ.

This applies also against any disease or calamity. Remember that the devil is seeking to destroy your soul and not your body, this is where the real battle is happening. God is promising divine protection for our souls.

11,12

"For he shall give his angels charge over thee, to keep thee in all thy ways.They shall bear thee up in *their* hands, lest thou dash thy foot against a stone. "

"God sends angels with special orders to protect you wherever you go, defending you from all harm. If you walk into a trap, they'll be there for you and keep you from stumbling. "

"for he will order his angels to care for you and guard you wherever you go. They will carry you in their hands, so that you won't trip on a stone. "

Angels are messengers from God, to be dispatched as a deputy. These angels are charged, commanded, appointed and given special orders by God Himself to act on His behalf.
Angels are given a divine command and are appointed by the God of hosts regarding us. There are angels around us who are sent by God for various missions and roles and please note that in this verse it is not one angel but many (angels)

*I have more than one angel watching over me
and protecting me in all my ways.*

I believe there are angels appointed by God for
my family; for my kids as they will accompany
them in their school bus and throughout their
day and during the night they are in their room
between their beds protecting them.
There are angels appointed for me and my wife
while we are driving and doing normal work and
house routines and while we are sleeping.
Several times I can testify that one of my family
members was protected in a strange way from
accidents. I have no logical explanation as to
why the car door did not fully open when my
younger kid tried opening it on the highway or
how a speedy car just missed him when he
decided to cross the street alone and the list goes
on.

The fact that we don't see those angels does not
deny their presence.
In the story of Elisha and his servant when their
city was surrounded by the enemy in order to
kill Elisha. His servant was so scared but Elisha
prayed that God would open his eyes to see who
were on their side in the spiritual realm and
when his eyes were opened, he saw armies of

angels...armies.

"When the servant of the man of God rose early in the morning and went out, behold, an army with horses and chariots was all around the city. And the servant said, "Alas, my master! What shall we do?" He said, "Do not be afraid, for those who are with us are more than those who are with them." Then Elisha prayed and said, "O LORD, please open his eyes that he may see." So the LORD opened the eyes of the young man, and he saw, and behold, the mountain was full of horses and chariots of fire all around Elisha."
2 Kings 6: 15-17

I was listening to a sermon by pastor Bill Johnson and he mentioned this story with a very interesting remark. He said that Elisha didn't get out to see the angels as he already knew they were there surrounding them and protecting them. He didn't need a physical proof. We usually neglect their presence or role but the Bible teaches us that they are there.

When I was writing this part something really interesting happened to me. I was sitting in a cafe' near my home drinking my usual coffee and focusing on writing and upon reaching this verse, I suddenly noticed the song that was playing in the cafe'. It was an oldie by the Swedish group ABBA and guess what was the title; "I believe in Angels "

For a moment I froze completely and smiled and I felt this was a message from God to emphasize to me the reality of angels around us.

I believe God has the highest sense of humor, after all He is the one who created it, and sometimes He would like to send us His messages through different and maybe funny ways.

The mission of the angels is to keep us in all our ways. Keep here means guard, protect and watch over. This is one of their missions; to protect those who dwell in Jesus in all their ways.

Hands in this verse are a symbol of power and ability. Angels are very powerful creatures and can do mighty things in both realms, the spiritual and the earthly. Remember when John saw an angel in the book of Revelation, he was scared because of the angel's might and appearance. Same thing happened with Daniel also.

Those angels are commanded to interfere and save us from any stumbling that may happen to us. Sometimes you will be prevented from doing

certain things or going into certain places because God knows it is not for your own good so He orders His angels to intercept your plans. They will change the course of things in order to protect us from any harm.
When we are fully submitted to God and obedient to the Holy Spirit within us, we are protected from any stumbling stones in our way.

Sometimes I wonder how I was saved from that accident or that incident and other times we experience miraculous things around us that changes our daily courses. These are acts of angels ordered by God.

John Gill put it this way regarding this verse: (**They shall bear thee up in their hands**,.... Which denotes the strength and power of angels to carry the saints in their hands; their tender care of them, such as a parent or nurse have of children; the helpless condition of the people of God, who are like infants, and need to be dealt with after this manner; the condescension of angels to take such an office on them, in submission to the will of God; the constant view they have of the saints, being always in their hands, and so in sight: thus they bear them)

Finally, and before we move to the next verse, I would like you to read this
comment by Adam Clarke which recaps many things:

(Let us remember that it is God, whose these angels are; He gives them charge and from Him they receive their commission, to Him they are responsible for their charge. From God thou art to expect them; and for their help He alone is to receive the praise. It is expressly said, He shall give his angels charge; to show that they are not to be prayed to nor praised but God alone, whose servants they are.)

All praise and thanks are to be to God alone and never to any angel. God is the one to be prayed to and worshiped and not any other spiritual being. We must neither neglect the role of the angles nor give them glory for what they are ordered to do. Glory is to be given only to God most high.

13

"Thou shalt tread upon the lion and adder: the young lion and the dragon shalt thou trample under feet. "

"You'll even walk unharmed among the fiercest powers of darkness, trampling every one of them beneath your feet. "

"You will tread down lions and snakes, young lions and serpents you will trample underfoot. "

The word lion here is not the one mentioned to describe God but used to describe the devil as he disguises himself as one.
"Be sober-minded; be watchful. Your adversary the devil prowls around like a roaring lion, seeking someone to devour. " 1 Pet. 5:8
Jesus is the real lion coming out of the tribe of Judah. The devil is pretending to be like a lion as he always wanted to be like God. This was his desire when he fell.
"How you are fallen from heaven, O Day Star, son of Dawn! How you are cut down to the ground, you who laid the nations low! You said in your heart, 'I will ascend to heaven; above the

stars of God I will set my throne on high; I will sit on the mount of assembly in the far reaches of the north; I will ascend above the heights of the clouds; I will make myself like the Most High " Isa. 14: 12-14

The adder is a kind of asp, venomous snake which is also a symbol of the devil.
Let us note what Adam Clarke said about it:
(The asp is a very small serpent, and peculiar to Egypt and Libya. Its poison kills without the possibility of a remedy. Those who are bitten by it die in about from three to eight hours; and it is said they die by sleep, without any kind of pain. Lord Bacon says the asp is less painful than all the other instruments of death.)

Sometimes the devil penetrates into our lives with his poisonous sins and it just takes over all of our lives. You may not feel it is something big but it is really deadly. You may gradually allow anger and resentment into your heart. Little problems with your spouse that are accumulating daily until they poison your whole lives both of you. A little compromise with sexual sins. A white lie at work and the list goes on.

Please beware of these sneaky and quiet attacks as they gradually spin their web around you until they finally strangle you and destroy your lives. Remember it s written: "and give no opportunity to the devil." Eph. 4:27

When we allow such small sins to enter our hearts, they just increase as an avalanche until we are overwhelmed by them.

Dragon in this verse is some sort of a monster. It is one of the devil's names.
Whether the enemy comes in a shape of lion with power, a snake sneaking around in silence or as a fearsome and terrible monster, we have complete victory through Jesus Christ.

Tread signifies the victory march as we walk over our enemies and claim new
territories while trample signifies the enemy's destruction. It means to crush something.
"Behold, I have given you authority to tread on serpents and scorpions, and over all the power of the enemy, and nothing shall hurt you"
Luke 10:19
We are not only protected form the evil spirits but we are to crush them under our feet and enjoy Jesus' victory on a daily basis. We are to

march in God's victorious army's march and
claim souls for Him all while treading over evil
spirits and crushing their powers over us and
over our brothers' and sisters'.

Jesus paid the full price on the cross and
defeated the devil for good and gave us this
victory and power. As Jesus did, we have the
right to crush the devil on his head and trample
over him.

14

"Because he hath set his love upon me, therefore
will I deliver him: I will set him on high,
because he hath known my name."

"For here is what the Lord has spoken to me:
Because you have delighted in me as my great
lover, I will greatly protect you. I will set you in
a high place, safe and secure before my face. "

"Because he loves me, I will rescue him;
because he knows my name, I will
protect him. "

In these last three verses, it is God who is
speaking now and not the psalmist. These are the
words of God now. God speaks to the man who:

   - Sets his love on God alone. His heart
belongs only to God and no one else.
   - Knows who God is, has a deep knowledge
and a close relationship with Him.

We cannot truly love someone unless we know
him/her well and when we do love we get to
know more because we delight in being with that

person.

Same applies in our relationship with God. When we get to know Him more and understand what's on His heart for us, we find ourselves loving Him more because we are delighted in the revelation we receive from Him.

It is all about the relationship, the intimate relationship with Him. Dwelling with Him. John understood this quite well and he always kept himself so close to Jesus.

This is the kind of relationship that God wants to have with us, intimate and close love relationship. To know Him and all that's on His heart. He delights to share what's inside of Him with you. He loves you more than any other person as He is your Maker and knows every little detail of your life even more than you do. He just longs to this relationship with you.

We were made, as a Church and also individuals, for such a close and intimate relationship with our Creator and Lover; to receive His abundant love and love Him back. We have the right to enjoy this relationship to the fullest, to receive God's love and rejoice. We are to rejoice every single day of our lives or else we are missing something really big.

"and as the bridegroom rejoices over the bride, so shall your God rejoice over you." Isa. 62: 5
"rejoice with joy unspeakable and full of glory" 1 Pet. 1:8
One of the fruits of the Spirit is Joy; people will see this joy in us and ask us about it.

But sometimes we are not living in this Joy.
Maybe because we never heard of such a right to live so.
Maybe we are just living an OK life.
Maybe due to many sins we have committed we are distant from God.
Or we might be extremely hurt, lonely, embarrassed, sad, depressed and even on the verge of desperation.
But there is good news. Look at this verse carefully:
"When I passed by you again and looked upon you, indeed your time was the time of _**love**_; so I spread My wing over you and covered your nakedness. Yes, I swore an oath to you and entered into a _**covenant**_ with you, and you became Mine," says the Lord God." Ezek. 16:8

God wants to enter in a Love Covenant with us.
God always makes the first move. Even if we

sometimes try hard to flee from Him or hide away, He still searches for us and takes the first move.

"Where can I go from your Spirit? Where can I flee from your presence? If I go up to the heavens, you are there; if I make my bed in the depths, you are there. If I rise on the wings of the dawn, if I settle on the far side of the sea, even there your hand will guide me, your right hand will hold me fast. If I say, "Surely the darkness will hide me and the light become night around me," even the darkness will not be dark to you; the night will shine like the day, for darkness is as light to you." Ps. 139:7-12

But God never forces Himself, it is still our choice to accept His move or reject it. It is our choice to enter the city of refuge or not.
He loves us even though we might be dirty, hurt, bleeding, looking ugly and miserable.
When we accept Him as our savior and Lord and enter into the only city of refuge, He then transforms us completely. This is His job to do. We just need to *surrender* and *accept* what He wants to change in us to become His beautiful bride. This is the work of the Holy Spirit inside our hearts.

"Then I bathed you with water and washed off your blood from you and anointed you with oil. I clothed you also with embroidered cloth and shod you with fine leather. I wrapped you in fine linen and covered you with silk. And I adorned you with ornaments and put bracelets on your wrists and a chain on your neck. And I put a ring on your nose and earrings in your ears and a beautiful crown on your head. Thus you were adorned with gold and silver, and your clothing was of fine linen and silk and embroidered cloth. You ate fine flour and honey and oil. You grew exceedingly beautiful and advanced to royalty. And your renown went forth among the nations because of your beauty, for it was perfect through the splendor that I had bestowed on you, declares the Lord God." Ezek. 16: 9-14

God cleanse us and anoints us with the Holy Spirit (water and oil) form all our sins, hurts and scars.
He covers our nakedness and shame and uses expensive and beautiful materials so that we may look and feel beautiful as well. He is the only one who can make us perfect in His image and as He planned before we were even born. God then crowns us and gives us precious jewelry to wear thus confirming our status as His

bride and the new Royal nature He bestows on us.
We were given fine and delicious food to eat and nurture, He supplies all our needs, physical, emotional and spiritual ones.

This is His goal for us: *You grew exceedingly **beautiful** and advanced to **royalty**.*
This is the true and real relationship that God wants us to be in with Him.

This is the exact same situation that Jesus spoke about in the proverb of the prodigal son. When the young son came back home, he was welcomed and not condemned, cleansed and clothed and a banquet was made for him. Love was in the air.
God wants us to enjoy a Romantic Covenant with Him.

To all the married couples out there, do you remember your engagement period?
You wanted to spend more time with your partner each day because you loved him/her and the longer you spent time together the more you loved each other and it continues through your marriage and each day.
This is not the topic here but remember that

marriage itself is not the final destination, it is a milestone on your journey together to love each other more and to know one another deeply.

Never stop learning more about your spouse and getting deeper in the relationship, never believe that there is nothing more to know or learn because when you reach this point, you will start declining.

We always need to be moving, either forward or backward but never to remain in the same place. To stop is to drop.

And in this process of an intimate relationship, you will understand yourself much better than before and hidden aspects of your life will be exposed and changed for your own best.

When we are in such a relationship with God, He will shed His light on some hidden parts in our personalities and some weaknesses to change these for our own good.

Remember that when you love someone you are vulnerable to that person.

I guess this is our best opportunity to be vulnerable in front of the only one who loves us unconditionally and never condemn us, our true heavenly Father.

Just read these verses to have a glimpse of His love

"Let him lead me to the banquet hall, and let his banner over me be _**love**_."
Song of Songs 2:4
"Many waters cannot quench _**love**_, nor can the floods drown it."
Song of Songs 8:7

Imagine the prodigal son we just spoke about. These verses perfectly describe what happened. Love is always the banner and nothing can separate us from or hold back God's love for us. Love is the heavenly kingdom's banner. What a great and cheerful news to know. I am so much grateful to this fact. Read these verses and allow the Holy Spirit to talk to you now.
"Who shall bring any charge against God's elect? It is God who justifies. Who is to condemn? Christ Jesus is the one who died— more than that, who was raised, who is at the right hand of God, who indeed is interceding for us. Who shall separate us from the love of Christ? Shall tribulation, or distress, or persecution, or famine, or nakedness, or danger, or sword? As it is written, "For your sake we are being killed all the day long; we are regarded as sheep to be slaughtered."
No, in all these things we are more than

conquerors through him who loved us.
For I am sure that neither death nor life, nor angels nor rulers, nor things present nor things to come, nor powers, nor height nor depth, nor anything else in all creation, will be able to separate us from the love of God in Christ Jesus our Lord." Rom. 8:33-39

Now back to our psalm verse, the usage of the word High here signifies exaltation, inaccessibly high.
God is promising to deliver us from any harm surrounding us and to put us in a very special place that is inaccessible to anyone else. A place of protection where we can can be safe from whatever is affecting others. A secret place.

Known here has the following meanings:
to know, learn to know, to perceive and see, find out and discern, discriminate, distinguish, know by experience, recognize, admit, acknowledge, confess, consider, be acquainted with.
We learn; this is a continuous process and we are to keep learning until the day that we finally see Him face to face. *We learn about Him from Him*. This learning is not theoretical one but a living one. As the disciples lived with Jesus and spent their days with Him learning from Him

and knowing Him more so we too should be doing so in our daily lives. By dwelling in the city of refuge, we are living each day with God and knowing Him in a deeper way.

We perceive; become aware and conscious of His presence in our lives and what He is doing in us and with us. Let's not be like the two disciples from Emmaus who didn't know that they spent a whole day with Jesus after His resurrection.

We are then able to discern and distinguish His voice and acts from ours or the devil's.

"But solid food is for the mature, for those who have their powers of discernment trained by constant practice to distinguish good from evil." Heb. 5:14

"My sheep hear my voice, and I know them, and they follow me." John 10:27

This is something that we grow in and build through the years. The more I listen to Him the better I will be able to distinguish His voice. Don't be afraid in the beginning if you fail in hearing God's voice or make a mistake obeying what you heard. We may not be sure if what we heard was from God, but unless it is something clearly against what the Bible teaches or what we know about God's nature and love then we need act in faith.

We learn from our failures much more than if we did not do anything at all.

God gave us wisdom also and we need to differentiate between certain things that were told to some people in specific times. If I say now that God called Peter to walk on water so I should do the same, I will drown. This was something specific to Peter only at that moment.

We experience God; we pass through many of situations and we build a deep knowledge and understanding from these experiences.

I had a very close friend when I was young and we used to meet up much and do many things together. Someday we were in a restaurant talking about many deep issues and then we both noticed that the person sitting next table was obviously eve dropping. Now my friend had a salad dish in front of him that he didn't finish and he looked at it and then to me. At this moment I was one hundred percent sure of what he was about to do and I said "Please don't, you will embarrass us "

I knew he would go to that person and offer him to join in this salad as he was practically hearing everything and intruding us. That was exactly what my friend did.

The point here is that by time and experience, you will get to know what's in the mind of your close friend without even the need of spoken words.

When we really know who God is and have this deep and intimate relationship with Him then we are lifted very high and delivered from any danger.

15

"He shall call upon me, and I will answer him: I *will be* with him in trouble; I will deliver him, and honour him. "

"I will answer your cry for help every time you pray, and you will find and feel my presence even in your time of pressure and trouble. I will be your glorious Hero and give you a feast "

"He will call on me, and I will answer him. I will be with him when he is in trouble. I will extricate him and bring him honor. "

God **ALWAYS** answers us when we call upon Him. Sometimes we may not discern His voice and sometimes the answer is delayed
Other times we can find the answer in an open opportunity, a specific person we meet, a Bible verse, a sermon, while we are praying, a closed door or any other way.
The CJB version states that God will answer our cry *every time* we pray. Not some times yes and others no. He is not busy or not paying attention to us. He promises to be always there and always listening to our prayers.

Remember when Elijah mocked the Baal's priests.

"And they took the bull that was given them, and they prepared it and called upon the name of Baal from morning until noon, saying, "O Baal, answer us!" But there was no voice, and no one answered. And they limped around the altar that they had made. And at noon Elijah mocked them, saying, "Cry aloud, for he is a god. Either he is musing, or he is relieving himself, or he is on a journey, or perhaps he is asleep and must be awakened." And they cried aloud and cut themselves after their custom with swords and lances, until the blood gushed out upon them. And as midday passed, they raved on until the time of the offering of the oblation, but there was no voice. No one answered; no one paid attention." 1 Kings 18: 26-29

But when Elijah called upon the living God, God answered with fire.

Now let me take some time here to dig a bit deeper in this topic. What really happens when we pray? When we are asking something according to God's will? The Bible teaches us the following: "Therefore I tell you, whatever you ask in prayer, believe that you have received it, and it will be yours." Mark 11:24

So we need to do two things in fact; Pray and Believe.

If we do these two, then we will be granted our prayers.
Now I am talking about all kinds of prayers and requests. From helping you in a small problem at work, satisfy that need, getting free from that bondage, healing that person, saving whole cities and the list goes on.
Remember when Abraham pleaded for Sodom and Gomorra, he was one hundred percent sure that God will grant him his request if there were those innocent people present there.

When we pray, God hears us and grants our request….immediately.
Let me put it this way: you make an order for a car with specific features. Once you place the order, the factory starts working on it immediately. It is entered into the production line but may take some time till it is completely finished.
Same case applies in the kingdom of heaven.
Your prayer is being processed in the assembly line once you have said amen.
The order for the answer was placed and granted by God when we prayed, if it is according to His

will. We need to just wait for it, wait in faith believing that we will get what we asked for because our God is a faithful one.

Many times we find an instant and immediate reply but why sometimes does it take time? Why not instantly always?
There are several reasons for this. Here are some:

-The devil is fighting back. This is exactly what happened to Daniel. "Then he said to me, "Fear not, Daniel, for from the first day that you set your heart to understand and humbled yourself before your God, your words have been heard, and I have come because of your words. The prince of the kingdom of Persia withstood me twenty-one days, but Michael, one of the chief princes, came to help me, for I was left there with the kings of Persia," Dan. 10:12,13
We can clearly see that God sent His angel with an answer to what Daniel was requesting from the first day that Daniel prayed but something happened in the spiritual realm that was not visible to Daniel. One of the enemy's demons who was in charge of the whole territory in the enemy's kingdom stood before God's angel and resisted him for three weeks so that the message

would not reach Daniel. So we need to learn to continue praying until we receive the answer, knowing that our prayer was heard and the answer was dispatched from the first day.

- God's timing. We always want the answer right now but God has a different opinion. God is outside time and He sees our whole future right now so He is the best one to determine when we should get what. Please don't be frustrated when there is a delay. Remember to trust in His perfect timings. Abraham had to wait till he was a hundred years old to get Isaac but he finally got him.

- Build my character. The answer may take some time also so as to build us up and equip us to deal with this prayer's answer. Imagine if you do not know how to drive and ask for a new car. What would happen if you get the car without being taught how to drive? You will not be able to use it or worse you will use it the wrong way and cause an accident. Same applies here. God uses the waiting time to shape us and change things in our personality to equip us for the prayer's answer.
He will give us an answer that is beyond our wildest dreams because we ask according to our

standards but He works according to His.
Finally, we will have peace in our hearts
regarding what we prayed for: the answer is on
its way and it is being perfectly prepared,
beyond any of our expectations.

Please beware that this applies to requests that
are in accordance to God's will. We need to be
ready and accepting a no for some requests that
are not in God's will or are not the best for us. I
believe that God is a loving father and a good
god. He will always do the best for us.

"For I know the plans I have for you, declares
the LORD, plans for welfare and not for evil, to
give you a future and a hope." Jer. 29:11

The main point here is that God answers us
especially when we call Him out of distress. We
need to hear and be sensitive to the Holy Spirit
to get all that's on His heart for us.

Though those around may be infected by the
troubles surrounding us, the person who abides
in God and make Him his city of refuge will be
in another position.

God Himself will deliver him and be his Hero.
My kids are big fans of the Avengers movies
and the idea of a super hero always fascinates
them. After all who does not like to have
someone like Iron Man, Thor, Spider Man,

Captain America, Black Widow…to be his own personal hero?

The bad news is these are all fictional characters and even if they were real, why should they be devoted to me or you in the first place? They should be always busy fighting some sort of super villain or saving the world from aliens.

But the good news is that you and me have a real hero, the only one and He is so personal. He is your heavenly father. He is the most mighty one and great in battles but always there for you only.

"Gird your sword on your thigh, O mighty one, in your splendor and majesty!"

Ps. 45:3

"Who is this King of glory? The LORD, strong and mighty, the LORD, mighty in battle!"

Ps. 24:8

The word honour here is a very beautiful one. It means to *be heavy*, that is in a good sense (*numerous, rich, honorable*) or to glorify.

God will not only deliver us from any evil but also honor us and bless us ABUNDANTLY and in a very RICH way.

In the Passion translation this blessing is descried as a *feast.* In a feast there is always plenty to have and much more than you desired or dared to dream about.

Just imagine what kind of feast God will throw for you.

"What no eye has seen, nor ear heard, nor the heart of man imagined, what God has prepared for those who love him" 1 Cor. 2:9

Remember what happened to the Israelites when getting out of Egypt. They got out with a fortune from the Egyptians.

"but each woman shall ask of her neighbor, and any woman who lives in her house, for silver and gold jewelry, and for clothing. You shall put them on your sons and on your daughters. So you shall plunder the Egyptians" Ex. 3:22

We will not only survive the bad times but will come out of them blessed and honored.

16

"With long life will I satisfy him, and shew him my salvation."

"You will be satisfied with a full life and with all that I do for you. For you will enjoy the fullness of my salvation. "

"I will satisfy him with long life and show him my salvation."

Life here is from an unused Hebrew word meaning to be hot. This means not just living and letting days pass by and getting older but a REAL life where there is something ALWAYS moving and ALIVE. Life with a meaning and a reason to be lived.
You may be living but not alive. You may be breathing, eating, sleeping and doing all normal physical activities, having a good job, healthy body, nice family but you may not have that flame inside of you that gives you the real perception of what it means to be alive.
This lack of reason is a main cause for depression and atheism in my opinion. You feel as if nothing matters and even your life itself has

no meaning. All is vain but this is not the real case. This is one of the famous lies through the ages that many have fallen for it.

Remember in Ecclesiastes, the write wrote these words in the beginning:

"Vanity of vanities, says the Preacher, vanity of vanities! All is vanity. What does man gain by all the toil at which he toils under the sun?" Eccles.1:2,3

Allow me to elaborate more, have you ever heard the song "The day before you came"? Now anyone who is a true ABBA fan will definitely relate to this song but for those who never heard about ABBA, let me to explain. ABBA was a Swedish singing band that was very popular in the 1980s and yes I know that's a bit old. They had many successful songs and many can remember the famous movie and musical "Mama Mia" some years ago. Both the play and the movie were based on their songs. Now they have a beautiful song called "The day before you came "

It is mainly a description of a typical day for someone from the moment she wakes up till she goes to bed again at night.

If you hear the song and read the lyrics you will

notice some themes about it that are hard to be missed; routine, lack of reason to live and emptiness of her life.

The singer describes in her daily activities details and how she is doing the same things over and over, day after day, in a very robotic, monotonous and routine way.

Nothing is **new** or **surprising**.....everything is so much **predictable** in her day.

Even the music of the song is in a very monotonous way adding to the feeling of repetition and routine.

These are some of the words that I would like to focus on:

"The **usual** place, the **usual** bunch "

"I must have **kept on dragging** through the business of the day without really knowing anything, I **hid a part of me away** "

"Oh yes, I'm sure my life was well within its **usual frame** the day before you came "

"It's funny, but I had no sense of **living without aim** the day before you came "

We are never told who this person is or how this meeting changed her life but the singer always says that everything was the same until she met this mysterious person.

When I first heard this song, I thought that it is a

perfect example regarding our lives before and after knowing Jesus. Let us examine it together:

We may be leading a very common and, by the world's standards, a good life.
Going to work/university/school each day via the same route, meeting the same people, drinking the same morning coffee, facing the same problems that we have been facing, eating the same type of food more or less, going to the gym and playing sports, reading the same newspapers and watching the same TV channels, updating our Facebook status and checking the latest Instagram pictures, doing the same activities with our spouses, kids or friends and then sleeping to start it all over again the next day.
There is absolutely nothing wrong in such a life but what is the aim of it and where are we heading to? Is life only meant to have fun in? Are our utmost goals a certain position, relationship, money, success…..only? Imagine that we reached our goals, then what?
The worst case is that we may be living a life of shame and guilt, due to several reasons, trying to survive each day and that becomes our sole aim.

Of course there are some who try to break the

normal daily routine by taking time off or doing anything differently but again we fall back into the same cycle sooner or later. Some may achieve higher humanity goals by helping others and serving the community which is great but still all of these activities will never fill the void deep inside our souls. We have a spiritual yearning and demand that can only be met in a spiritual way.

The main point is not only in the activities but the meaning of life as a whole.
The singer kept saying "everything was the same the day before you came "
I tend to understand that things went differently after that day. I hope so.
The same I believe applies to our lives after we meet Jesus a real meeting.

Let's look at a couple of people who met Jesus and see whether their lives truly changed or not and into which direction:

1- Peter:
Peter was a fisherman and maybe a good one but his life was so monotonous in my opinion. He would wake up, clean the nets and straighten them, fix the torn ones, go out with his

workmates to catch fish, return to sell them and eat the rest then go back home to repeat it all over again the next day. Nothing was new, everything was more or less predictable. Everything was within the usual frame.

Does this look familiar to "The **usual** place, the **usual** bunch "

Did Peter had to **keep dragging** through the business of the day? I think so.

Did he ever wonder "What is the purpose of all of this? Shall I be doing this forever till I die? "

Bear in mind that this was quite a *Normal* life and maybe a successful one as well. Nothing wrong in it by the way but what was the **aim** of such a life?

2- The Samaritan Woman:
This woman was a prostitute. She was well known in the city and no one accepted her at all to the point that she had to go fetch her water at specific times when she could meet nobody at the well. She got used to be taken advantage of by men and her life was a repeated cycle of torture, shame and feeling of unworthiness each time she slept with someone. I am sure she had low or zero self-esteem.

She reminds me of Fantine from the movie "Les Miserables" when she sang
"Don't they know they're making love to one already dead! "

She got used to this type of life and even stopped seeking a better one. Nothing was new, everything was more or less predictable.
She got used to **usual** place and **usual** men.
She also **kept dragging** through painful days, wishing death and daring not to dream about redemption.
She definitely **hid** many parts away and locked them in her heart. People see a certain personality that is not the real her.
And finally, I highly doubt that she had any **aim** in such a life.

I can go on and on about other people who had a routine life, whether it was a good one or bad one, meeting Jesus and whatever happened to them the next moment, and not next day, after they met Him.
So for these two examples, did their way of living changed or not and if yes then in which way?
Let us examine first Peter's life.
As we saw, he led a very normal and probably a

good life according to the word's standards back then. But the moment he met Jesus, his whole world turned upside down literally.

Let us note the first thing Jesus said to him:
"And Jesus, walking by the sea of Galilee, saw two brethren, Simon called Peter, and Andrew his brother, casting a net into the sea: for they were fishers. And he saith unto them, Follow me, and I will make you fishers of men. And they straightway left their nets, and followed him." Matt. 4:18-20

Why would someone leave all he has built and been doing for years and decide to follow someone whom he has just met?

How can he leave behind all his securities, experiences and things he knew so much for something that he definitely didn't understand (fishers of men)?

According to the world's standards, this must have been a very silly and immature thing to do but I believe that Peter hearing Jesus and looking into His eyes, knew deep inside his heart that this is the thing he had been looking for and searching all of his life, the real aim of his life.

Jesus said: "I am the way, and the truth, and the life. No one comes to the Father except through

me." John 14:6
Peter finally found the thing that he was missing. From that moment, Peter began experiencing life in a much different way. One day he would be healing sick people, another day expelling demons or even walking on water once.
His life became everything but predictable or monotonous.
I can hear Peter waking up each day, so excited about what this day will bring in his journey with Jesus. Even his name was changed from Simon to Peter.

Please note that from the day that you know Jesus and accepts Him in your life as your savior and Lord, He will speak upon you and appoint you a new name for His kingdom.
Each one of us has a new name waiting for us to know it and live by it. This would be our true identity that God had in mind before we were even born.
Remember, God is your father and as a father, He has the right to give you your name, your real identity name.

The second example is the Samaritan woman. Upon knowing whom she was talking to, this woman did two things.

"So the woman left her water jar and went away into town and said to the people, Come, see a man who told me all that I ever did. Can this be the Christ?" John 4:28,29

She first left her bucket at the well. She completely forgot what she was there for in the first place. Well, I guess this is the Jesus effect. She was overwhelmed by Him and how He knew everything about her yet He did not condemn her. He showed her love and acceptance, two things she yearned for every day in her life.

Once we meet Jesus, we forget our routine and normal lives and we get really excited by who He is and what He might do in our lives.

The second thing she did was running into the city and telling everyone about Jesus. How He told her everything she had done and that He must be the long awaited Messiah.

She was not ashamed anymore. For the first time probably in years she could walk among people unashamed and not only this, but proclaim that she was a sinner but finally met Jesus.

She finally didn't hide anymore. She did not need her masks anymore. She didn't hide physically but most importantly she didn't hide her true self. She was transformed into a new person. She became sort of a missionary. Who could believe such a thing.

Whoever says that living with God is boring has never tried if for real.
Some try to stereotype such a life as weak and marginal, only fit for losers. Well, the Bible contradicts such picture completely.
 Imagine one day you can walk on water, the other you raise someone from the dead. Another day you feed thousands of men, women and children using few loaves of bread and fish.
Above all imagine being in real and deep fellowship with God, hearing Him daily and enjoying His presence.
This doesn't look like a boring, predictable, weak or powerless life at all.
New life EACH day, nothing is predictable with Jesus.

In C.S.Lewis' wonderful series "The Chronicles of Narnia" Aslan says to Lucy "Things never happen the same way twice."

Always remember that you are following the Creator. God loves to do new things each day.

Still not everyone who met Jesus decided to follow Him, many may resist change, even if it was for their best. Their lives have also changed but unfortunately it did towards the wrong side.

In the wonderful movie, "The Shawshank Redemption". In this movie the prisoners got so used to the prison walls that when one was set free, he couldn't make it and killed himself. Whether it was fear from change, dependency on own strength and not wanting to let go or not believing that there is a chance of redemption, many have turned their back to Jesus. So please open the door to Him and allow Him to change your whole life. You will not need to hide anything anymore and will be free to be yourself, the original version, so that there is a new beginning since the day He came.

Let us get back to our verse now.
Satisfy here means to have in excess. This is similar to the previous verse where honor meant heavy. Also the word salvation here means welfare, prosperity.
Whoever lives in the shelter of the Most High shall see the goodness of God and experience His great power. He will experience life in its fullness and true meaning.

"I came that they may have life and have it abundantly" John 10:10

So this is what it means to dwell and live in the one and only city of refuge; Jesus.

Made in the USA
Middletown, DE
19 August 2021